THE AUTOMATION ADVANTAGE

This book is a practical guide for how to make an impact and realize value from automation. There is a strong focus on the real-world execution of an automation strategy that makes it an accessible must-read for both a business management and technology audience.

—MIKE CRISAFULLI, SVP of Software Engineering at Comcast

Consistently creating value with technology is hard. *The Automation Advantage* makes it simple. The authors lay out a comprehensive path using modern techniques that will be appreciated by both the thinker and the practitioner.

—MARK SPYKERMAN, Chief Information Officer of
AmerisourceBergen

The pandemic has required businesses to hit the fast-forward button on adopting technology while becoming agile enough to be ready for what emerges next. *The Automation Advantage* couldn't have come at a better time, providing a comprehensive road map to launch automation and AI initiatives at scale and accelerating technology-driven transformation.

—PAUL DAUGHERTY, Group Chief Executive – Technology
and Chief Technology Officer of Accenture
and coauthor of *Human+Machine*

A brilliant field manual for the coming Automation Age.

—RICHARD D'AVENI, Bakala Professor of Strategy at
Tuck School of Business at Dartmouth College
and author of *The Pan-Industrial Revolution*

As with any transformation effort, getting your people to embrace change can be challenging. *The Automation Advantage* clearly identifies common myths and barriers and how they can be addressed through a human-centric approach. This is *not* a book of strategy. It's a book of execution that will enable your organization with actions to take in order to succeed.

—ANDY NALLAPPAN, Chief Technology Officer of Broadcom

Successful intelligent automation requires you to get more than just the technology right. *The Automation Advantage* addresses this clearly and effectively by providing the guiding principles and steps for changing your organization's technology, governance, culture, and even leadership style.

—CHARLENE LI, entrepreneur, speaker, and *New York Times* bestselling author of *The Disruption Mindset*

The authors cut through the hype to explore why automation is the necessary discipline to ensure your processes provide the data—at speed—to achieve your business outcomes. *The Automation Advantage* takes us on a refreshing journey that aligns how enterprise operations leaders need to approach automation and AI in the virtual economy.

—PHIL FERSHT, CEO and Chief Analyst of HFS Research

A great book, with ample examples of automation at work. It cements all the ideas and discussions I have had on this topic with the expert automation team at Accenture.

—RAJIV KAKAR, Group Chief Information Officer of Thai Union

A CIO needs vision, leadership, and the technical nous to execute successfully. A world with zero human-touch application maintenance is absolutely attainable—a world with self-healing and self-configuring systems powered by AI. *The Automation Advantage* sets out a strategic approach to getting there, from both a technology and human perspective.

—ED ALFORD, Chief Technology Officer of New Look

We are entering a world of autonomous enterprises where analytics, automation, and AI converge. *The Automation Advantage* definitively shows how organizations can improve decision velocity and precision decisions.

—R "RAY" WANG, CEO of Constellation Research and
author of *Everybody Wants to Rule the World*

THE
AUTOMATION
ADVANTAGE

THE
AUTOMATION
ADVANTAGE

EMBRACE THE FUTURE OF PRODUCTIVITY AND IMPROVE SPEED, QUALITY, AND CUSTOMER EXPERIENCE **THROUGH AI**

**BHASKAR GHOSH
RAJENDRA PRASAD
GAYATHRI PALLAIL**
OF ACCENTURE

New York Chicago San Francisco Athens London Madrid
Mexico City Milan New Delhi Singapore Sydney Toronto

1 2 3 4 5 6 7 8 9   LCR   26 25 24 23 22 21

ISBN   978-1-260-47329-2
MHID   1-260-47329-5

e-ISBN   978-1-260-47330-8
e-MHID   1-260-47330-9

Library of Congress Cataloging-in-Publication Data

Names: Ghosh, Bhaskar, author. | Prasad, Rajendra, author. | Pallail, Gayathri, author.
Title: The automation advantage : embrace the future of productivity and improve speed, quality, and customer experience through AI / Bhaskar Ghosh, Rajendra Prasad, and Gayathri Pallail.
Description: New York : McGraw Hill, [2021] | Includes bibliographical references and index.
Identifiers: LCCN 2021031379 (print) | LCCN 2021031380 (ebook) | ISBN 9781260473292 (hardback) | ISBN 9781260473308 (ebook)
Subjects: LCSH: Automation—Management. | Artificial intelligence—Industrial applications. | Strategic planning.
Classification: LCC HD45.2 .G496 2021 (print) | LCC HD45.2 (ebook) | DDC 658/.0563—dc23
LC record available at https://lccn.loc.gov/2021031379
LC ebook record available at https://lccn.loc.gov/2021031380

To the memory of all Accenture employees
who lost their lives fighting Covid-19

CONTENTS

FOREWORD

by Julie Sweet, CEO of Accenture

The Covid-19 pandemic made it very clear that technology is a lifeline for economies, governments, organizations, and people. It not only helped us solve immediate challenges and stay connected with one another—it also changed the way we see and understand the world.

Automation, the focus of this insightful and extremely practical book, is no small part of this change. Like many other technologies, automation advanced greatly over the past decade with the rise of intelligent systems—encompassing capabilities like applied artificial intelligence (AI), industrial and process robotics, and service robots. Now, due to the impact of the pandemic, the pace of automation innovation is moving much faster than we anticipated.

There is no better guide to automation than Bhaskar Ghosh, Accenture's chief strategy officer and former group chief executive of Accenture Technology Services. I have worked with him for many years, and his invaluable vision and counsel have helped countless companies through their digital transformations. In *The Automation Advantage*, Bhaskar and his coauthors, Rajendra Prasad and Gayathri Pallail, draw on their veteran expertise to explain how automation works—and how it works best. They cut through myths and misunderstandings to blaze a clear trail for any business leader looking to develop an automation strategy, create new value, and realize growth—all with a human-centric approach.

Because like all technologies, automation should never be considered in isolation—it's always in the context of solving human problems. I often tell other CEOs that if someone comes to them and says, "I have an automation project" or "I have a blockchain initiative," they should say, "No." They shouldn't even ask what it is, because no initiative should ever start with technology. Ultimately, technology enables; it's about empowering *people*.

Currently, we estimate that we are at only 15 to 20 percent of what could be automated. We're going to see that percentage rapidly increase, as automation continues to spread from manual processes, such as building cars in a factory, to enhancing mental processes, such as giving a consumer a consistently better customer experience. Automation is helping companies actively grow their businesses through speed, safety, quality, cost-efficiency, and resilience.

Seizing this opportunity, companies are investing in this technology and creating jobs. But are people ready and able to fill them? Are young people leaving high school with basic technology skills and digital literacy? The answer in many cases is no. Before the pandemic, we were not ready to address the growing global reskilling need that automation is bringing. Unfortunately, we still are not prepared. As companies, we have a huge responsibility to reskill, and it is imperative that we bring together government, educational institutions, and not-for-profits with equal speed to partner on addressing this need.

As we enter the postpandemic era, we are seeing a world awakened to an incredible opportunity to reimagine and rebuild responsibly and sustainably. Instead of seeing automation as a technology that competes with people for jobs, it can and should be considered a way to contribute to our shared success. By eliminating mundane and repetitive tasks, automation allows us to focus human attention where it's most needed—on creativity, empathy, and critical thinking. *The Automation Advantage* helps us understand not only how automation can create value for a business but also how its unique combination of technology and human ingenuity can play a part in transforming the global economy into one that works for the benefit of all.

PREFACE

Sharing What Works

The year is 2019, and the place is a beautifully furnished meeting room in a modern office tower—the headquarters of a global company. We've come to town to meet with a management team considering a complex operational business issue, which we think presents a great opportunity for intelligent automation. We're confident we can make a case for this with the information we've assembled, which anticipates the questions these executives will probably have.

First, they'll likely ask: "What is intelligent automation?"

Answer: It's the new era of automation in which machines are used to perform tasks formerly reserved for humans—tasks that involve analyzing data, making decisions, and learning from what follows once decisions are implemented.

Second, they'll ask: "Why should we invest in automation like this—will it really make us a better company?"

Answer: Your competitive edge will still depend, more than ever, on your people's talents, but you'll be able to leverage and augment those talents to an unprecedented level.

Third: "Are other companies in our industry already moving in this direction—and is it paying off?"

Answer: Yes. (We've done our research.)

Finally, they'll ask, "Given our other priorities, why is now the right time to invest?"

But as the meeting begins, the surprise is on us. These aren't the questions the executives ask.

As we share our thoughts on known pain points in their type of business and how automation could help, the executives are already nodding and pushing us along. This is a group already convinced that the opportunities are exceptional. It turns out there have been pockets of experimentation going on in their organization, and these limited, one-off solutions have been yielding seriously good results. So this top team wants to take things to the next level.

They're past the *why* questions and well into the *how*. As they aim to approach the automation opportunity at scale, they want to know where to start. How to identify top business cases and how to determine the priority order in which to address them. How to assess their legacy systems and data issues that might delay them. They also wonder how they can be sure their people—both the technology staff and the business users of the new tools—will value the change and want to be part of it.

It turned out to be the best boardroom conversation we'd had all year, as we found ourselves talking excitedly about the very issues consuming us personally at that moment. We'd been working with a variety of leading companies that had reached the same "scaling" point in their intelligent automation journeys, and we had been able to identify important patterns, the common pitfalls, and the clever solutions that cut across their companies.

As a technology consulting team with a practice area to lead, we had been pulling together these lessons and trying to distill them into practical guidance on designing and implementing successful automation projects. Now, the observations were jelling into insights that we knew could genuinely accelerate an organization's progress.

And guess what: the following month, we had a very similar conversation with another company's management team, also jumping ahead to the "how" questions—and then a great workshop with yet another right after that. We found ourselves repeating key messages and refining them, figuring out how best to organize and articulate the principles we were developing in practice. Eventually, we felt like we had covered all the major bases and developed a point of view on each of them, whether in a white paper, blog post, speech, methodology module, or presentation deck—however, we felt we should really pull them together into one coherent package. One of us named the challenge at that point: "That would require a whole book." And here we are.

The book you hold in your hand is designed to answer that smart set of burning questions we continue to be asked by managers and leaders who want to proceed quickly and confidently in automation initiatives. But if we're setting the whole context for how this book came about, we also have to mention that other big source of pressure that hit organizations all around the world in 2020—much as we might all want to forget it. We were well into the process of writing the book when Covid-19 hit, and we, our company, and all our clients found ourselves struggling to protect our people, help our customers, and remain productive amid a devastating pandemic.

We know and work with many academics, management gurus, and analysts focused on the realm of intelligent automation, and sometimes we envy their situations. For some of them, a lockdown on global travel and orders to work from home made this a year when they suddenly had more capacity to reflect and write. For us, it was a crazy time of demand for client solutions, as automation became more important than ever. This was an urgent realization by many firms.

As early as April 2020, *Information Age* reported that HFS Research surveyed 631 major enterprises about how they anticipated the pandemic would affect their strategies and operations. One of its questions asked: "How do you expect Covid-19 to impact your spending" in 10 major areas of technology investment. Fully 55 percent of respondents knew already that their spending on automation would increase, making this the second most reported increase after cybersecurity—both obvious concerns as so much mission-critical work moved abruptly to online platforms.[1]

For us, the challenges came simultaneously on many fronts—in our client projects, every one of which is unique, and also within our own company. Accenture itself moved instantly to new modes of staying productive—away from the consulting industry norm by which professionals spend the bulk of their time on-site at client locations and generate much of their value through in-person working sessions. The companies we had already been helping with automation seemed most eager to double down on that work. For companies seeking hyper-automation before (where discrete automated tasks roll up into seamlessly automated processes, and automated analysis identifies for itself new opportunities to take automation into new realms), the pandemic crisis pushed those ambitions further.

Having a book to complete in the midst of all this was not what we had anticipated when we signed the contract with our publisher. Yet there was a silver lining, too. We think the fact that we were so deeply in the mode of capturing and explaining principles from real-world engagements made it easier for us to make sense of this new, very dynamic, and frankly unnerving situation.

In many ways, this book represents the synthesis of long experience. The real veteran among us is Bhaskar Ghosh, who has spent a career as an automation advocate and been responsible for many groundbreaking solutions. He and "RP," as all of Rajendra Prasad's friends and colleagues call him, have worked together on many of these, ranging from small projects to large transformations. Since then, often with Gayathri Pallail leading the charge, we have helped many clients apply intelligent automation to remove pain points in risk management, sales strategy, customer service, and more.

As Accenture's work in this area increased, we also found ways to make our own company's internal processes more effective using automation solutions like workflow systems. The human factor is also critical. We've approached our internal automation opportunities with creativity, empathy, and innovation in the spirit of keeping the human advantage front and center for organizations we work with. In any situation where people must solve a complex problem, we're convinced they can do it better if augmented by robust automation.

Along the way, we've seen our colleagues make many technical and managerial breakthroughs. In fact, as we began work on this book, the news came that Accenture had just been granted its 60th patent related to intelligent automation. To us, this is a real point of pride. We noted already that we stay close to the discoveries being made by leading researchers in universities, startups, and research and development labs. The work they do is invaluable to us. But meanwhile, our great privilege is that we are able to innovate in the setting of a global professional services company where we work with the world's largest and most sophisticated companies. Their managers and leaders are inspirational. They are eager to get real innovation done. The problems they need to solve matter to their success and to the world.

Working where we do also means that we benefit from a culture that prizes discovery—and the documentation and dissemination of it to the world. This is evident from the constant stream of forward-looking research that Accenture publishes in every form imaginable—from podcasts to survey reports to high-level strategy books. In a company that invests heavily in staying at the cutting edge, it is a cultural value that we should have research-backed perspectives to offer our clients and other stakeholders.

But while we earn our patents for inventions that are specialized and technology focused, it's critical that our client-serving teams can connect those with the problems of clients, even when the client involved is dealing with a highly strategic issue and talking in very big-picture terms. To our people, it may be clear that the patented tool or technique directly contributes to the client solution, but it isn't always obvious to others. A book like this can equip more people in the business world with the story line that explains why this fast-evolving intelligent automation technology is so important to achieve business objectives, and what it takes to put it in place, at scale.

To be clear, this is not a strategy book—it's an execution book. Our self-assigned mission was to produce a truly practical guide. So yes, we devote an opening chapter to offering some historical context on automation and making the case for why it is now the time to invest in cognitive technologies—but we then move quickly into content relevant to organizations who already sense there is a big opportunity and want to translate that enthusiasm into action.

We identify the most common barriers to acting on that sense in Chapter 2, as a way of setting up the value of what follows; all of it is geared toward overcoming these obstacles. In Chapter 3, we emphasize the need to be clear on strategic intent because a shared commitment to the business priorities is the necessary North Star to guide every aspect of planning and implementation. This strategic imperative segues directly into Chapter 4, which focuses on how to choose wisely from the seemingly endless opportunities most organizations face to automate some activity or another. Hint: it has as much to do with overall capability building and intelligent automation maturity as with the potential bottom-line impact of individual solutions.

Throughout, we place emphasis on what it takes to derive the highest value from investments, and we address very ground-level problems and considerations. In Chapter 5, we explain how to map out an implementation plan, put governance in place, and keep track of progress. In Chapter 6, we get into technology discussions on how to architect a future-proof automation—at a level that is understandable to not just the technology team, but also other functional executives and general managers. In Chapter 7, we discuss the "soft stuff" that all experienced leaders know is really the hard stuff: change management, reskilling, organizational culture, and other elements of people management. At a high level, we underscore the takeaway advice at the end of each chapter, but we urge you to delve deep into the stories that bring the advice to life and the research findings that back up its validity. Our objective in the text has been to write to that all-important midlevel that helps the most strategic thinkers in organizations understand the art of the possible and helps the most focused tool builders and technologists make the connections between their work and the overall strength and agility of the enterprise.

As you'll see, the metaphor and concept of a road map turns out to be very important to that overall success. It gets introduced early and reiterated often. Chapter 8 emphasizes that this is not a journey that has an end; there is always effort required to sustain and build on the gains—and without that effort, there's a real risk of backsliding. Finally, Chapter 9 gives a glimpse of where the journey may take organizations in the future, as they use automation to achieve new levels of relevance, responsibility, and resilience.

Our hope is that, with this book, we are putting a valuable map into your hands. It reflects the long road we have taken, as we learned from years of complex business challenges, and then the crisis of a global pandemic, as we helped our most sophisticated clients transform from manual operations to automated (and in some cases hyperautomated) ones. But now it is your map to keep drawing, as you embark on your organization's own intelligent automation journey. We wish you every success on it. We are happy if our experience can provide some guideposts along the way—and we look forward to learning more from what you are able to achieve.

ACKNOWLEDGMENTS

We are grateful to our colleagues for believing in the idea of capturing our automation experiences and sharing them with readers. We would like to thank all the experts and thought leaders who contributed to this book's success.

We extend special thanks to Julie Sweet, CEO of Accenture, for supporting us as we wrote this book and for her vision and leadership in making a difference in this new world through intelligent automation. Her conviction in the advantage of automation has been a constant source of inspiration for us.

Our gratitude and sincere thanks to Accenture's technology leader, Paul Daugherty, for believing in the value of this book and for providing his thought leadership, wisdom, and guidance throughout the process.

Deepest thanks to Julia Kirby who, with a brilliant editorial mind, played a crucial role in the book's development. Julia dedicated many hours over the past two years to help us turn our ideas and thinking into outlines and finally into compelling chapters.

We owe special thanks to the many visionaries and extraordinary leaders at Accenture who took the time to read each draft and provide feedback to enrich the narrative. We are grateful to Kelly Bissell, Gregory Douglass, Kishore Durg, Edy Liongosari, Nirav Sampat, Rahul Varma, and Sanjeev Vohra. Thanks also to Francis Hintermann for not only reading the manuscript but also offering additional insights based on his extensive experience and research findings.

Throughout this journey, we were advised by Accenture marketing pros Kathleen Bellah and Raghavendra Rao, who helped us fine-tune our message. Kathleen generously read drafts and helped hone both strategic concepts and minute details. We are incredibly grateful to the rest of the marketing team, especially to Ed Maney for his dedication to this project throughout. Ed has worked with us week in, week out to make this book a reality. Likewise, Linda King has been an unfailing support to the project. Ed and Linda have been indispensable throughout the process from beginning to end, meticulously executing their work and providing guidance and encouragement. Special thanks also goes to Nancy Goldstein for bringing her marketing and communication expertise to bear to ensure the success of the book.

Huge thanks to the team at our publisher, McGraw Hill, led by Casey Ebro. Their support for the concept was unwavering, and they played a vital role in helping shape and refine the manuscript.

Our gratitude also extends to the many pioneering clients who have trusted Accenture to be their partner in their automation journey. We've had the unique privilege not only to research the ideas in this book but also to apply the concepts and observe the results as we worked with these true pioneers in this digital age.

We are blessed to have a brilliant team of automation leaders who have, day in and day out, implemented the concepts and ideas in this book with our many clients. Special thanks to Koushik Vijayaraghavan, Aditi Kulkarni, and Luke Higgins for the enthusiasm and passion with which they drive automation maturity for clients who have partnered with Accenture.

And finally, on a more personal note:

Bhaskar Ghosh: I'd like to thank my wife, Arpita, for all her support, encouragement, and inspiration for my work over the decades and for tolerating my long working hours on evenings, weekends, and sometimes also during vacations. Thanks also to my two sons, Anirban and Anindya, for their endless encouragement for this book.

Rajendra Prasad: I want to thank my wife, Kavitha, for her continued encouragement and support during my entire career. My two daughters, Janvi and Keerthana, help cheer me up every day with lots of fun. I also want to thank my mom, Saroja Devi, who first taught me how to write short articles during my school days.

Gayathri Pallail: I would like to thank my husband, Rajesh, for being unconditionally supportive at every step of my personal and professional journey. I'm especially thankful to my children, Ritvik and Anika, for putting up with me throughout this journey. Special thanks to my parents (Krishnadas and Jayanthi) and my parents-in-law (Ramadasan and Bhagyalakshmi) for all the support they have given me throughout my career.

The Intelligence Imperative

A few years ago, one of Italy's leading daily regional newspapers, *Il Secolo XIX*, introduced a new form of automation to its operations that, to some eyes, seemed audacious.

As a large, for-profit business serving a mass market, *Il Secolo* already depended on automation in many forms. The very genesis of its business was one of the most impactful automation technologies in history—the printing press—and more recently, it had transformed itself around the internet and digital technology. In fact, *Il Secolo* has long been one of the most forward-thinking papers in Italy, having pioneered color printing, integrated newsrooms, multichannel digital presence, and social media engagement.

This new automation project, however, struck some as moving in a dramatically different direction. This time, the tasks being automated were part of the intellectual work of *journalists*—the highly educated and creative workers at the very heart of *Il Secolo*'s premium product.

Like many newspapers, *Il Secolo* faced serious challenges. The number of readers was contracting and revenues were dropping. The leadership at *Il Secolo XIX* understood that sustaining and growing a loyal readership meant continuously rethinking what it means to be a newspaper. And doing so at the nonstop pace of a modern 24/7/365 newsroom. They realized they needed to find new ways to produce cost-effective, high-quality journalism to increase digital traffic, reader loyalty, and company revenues.

The solution?

A virtual assistant that would boost its writers' and editors' productivity, without compromising quality. Consisting of artificial-intelligence-infused software, the virtual assistant was designed to leverage human talents and streamline the process of producing digital content.[1]

Now, when a journalist starts a story, the assistant continuously checks the text for data consistency, potential links to other sources, as well as spelling and syntax. By offering journalists prompts to other content it thinks will be relevant, whether from previous stories or external resources, the assistant gives journalists a completely new way to check sources, develop background understanding, and—more important—add extra content they might have otherwise missed.

Far from feeling threatened by their new, virtual colleague, workers in *Il Secolo*'s newsroom welcomed the support. In six months, every journalist on staff was using the technology. Many of *Il Secolo*'s journalists found the virtual assistant not only saved time but also stimulated new thoughts, prompting them to consider different angles, enriching their understanding, and revealing nonobvious connections to other stories already published or in the works.

At the enterprise level, the virtual assistant is translating strategy to reality. More abundant, high-quality content provides more opportunities to attract advertising and to grow revenues with digital subscriptions.[2] *Il Secolo*'s success story is just one of many unfolding today under the broad banner of *intelligent automation*. It is a good case to start with because it has all the basic elements of the much wider trend.

Intelligent automation involves the application of smart machines, taking advantage of the various technologies that are collectively referred to as artificial intelligence (AI). It applies these tools to work performed by knowledge workers—a realm that has long been resistant to automation. And it calls for intelligent management of the automation process, to ensure uptake by the organization, to deploy the resources available for automation to the highest-value opportunities, and to integrate the new solution into a richly interconnected business system.

In *Il Secolo*'s case, automating a piece of the content creation workflow had implications for printing timelines, editorial assignments, ad sales, page layouts, and even human resources planning. All these elements had to be considered to create a coherent, structured plan.

Like many great newspapers around the world, *Il Secolo* regularly reports on advances in AI. One recent story, for example, highlighted software made by the American company Affectiva and the Japanese company Empath that is designed to detect people's emotions. Perhaps aided by the virtual assistant, the article referenced the name of a famous science fiction story of the 1960s: *Do Androids Dream of Electric Sheep?* If it was possible to speculate in the 1960s, the reporter noted in the story, that computers were capable of unconscious cognitive activity, then maybe we shouldn't be surprised that they could evolve to pick up on the unspoken feelings of others around them.

But even as reporters in this news organization have their eyes on the future of intelligent automation, they are, in their own jobs, making practical use of it very much in the present. They are part of a traditional business moving headlong into the digital age, reinventing itself to continue to thrive.

Automation's New Era

Automation is not a very old word: it was coined less than 75 years ago, when a Ford engineering manager named Del Harder named the department that would oversee the company's growing research and experimentation in replacing assembly-line workers with machines. Essentially, Harder took the noun *automaton*—meaning a robot or other type of self-operating mechanism—and turned it into the verb *to automate*. The term took off as fast as the technology. Automating work was a breakthrough productivity changer when it arrived in big industrial corporations in the mid-twentieth century.[3]

To be sure, the much earlier machines of the Industrial Revolution—starting with spinning jennies, power looms, water frames, and such—also represented automation, even if the term was not yet in use. But it was the scale attained by industrial businesses by the 1940s that turned automation into a discipline and constant quest.

Mass production facilities made the economics of designing, engineering, and deploying capital equipment attractive in a way they had never been before. As at Ford, the focus across industries was on making manufacturing processes faster and cheaper—as well as safer and more capable of producing consistent quality—by substituting machine power for human labor.

Workers had always used tools, but automation meant handing work over to a tool itself.

By the turn of the millennium, machinery was pervasive across industrial settings, reducing to a fraction the former effort that had been required to produce goods. Automation had fully advanced into its next era.

If there is a single biggest story to be told about the transformation of the world's leading economies over the twentieth century, it's about their shift from being manufacturing-based to being service-based. Data from the US Bureau of Labor Statistics shows that, after a wartime high in 1943, employment in the nation's manufacturing sector has dropped nearly constantly. As a share of total employment, manufacturing accounted for 37.9 percent of jobs in 1943. In 2018, it accounted for just 8.5 percent of jobs. Meanwhile, service jobs—first largely in retail and more recently in healthcare and social assistance—skyrocketed.

Today (and since the end of 2017), healthcare accounts for the largest number of jobs in the US economy, followed closely by the retail trade.[4] With this shift came a growing awareness that the services economy, too, consisted of much repetitive, standardized labor—and a sense that automation could reduce the amount of human labor in services, just as it had done in manufacturing.

In banking, for example, Barclays Bank asked some 50 years ago: Could we automate the bulk of a teller's work? And the ATM—the automated teller machine—was born. Within a decade, retailers spotted their own opportunity, and a grocery store in Troy, Ohio, made history in 1974 with the first barcode scan of a product (it was a pack of Wrigley's Juicy Fruit gum).[5]

The questions have since become more ambitious. In healthcare, for example: Could automation make diagnosis of maladies quicker and more accurate? Could the ability to analyze trillions of data points across a patient population lead to more evidence-based treatments? Could surgeons be assisted in real time by virtual agents monitoring patient vital statistics and performing on-the-spot pathology? The healthcare system, with its many inefficiencies and an extreme need for best-practice performance, would seem to be ripe for much more automation—but only if the automation is intelligent.

This wave of automation was not limited, moreover, to those companies designated by government statisticians as "service providers" versus "manufacturers." Even within manufacturing companies, because they had so thoroughly automated their production processes, payrolls were newly dominated by knowledge workers.[6] Even at companies traditionally known as manufacturers, there are armies of people performing back-office and front-office roles, whose jobs consist mainly of information processing, greatly outnumbering the human beings on the shop floors.

We are now in the newest era of automation, when it's clear that much of the office work that computers have enabled people to do more productively can actually be computerized. Whereas in the past, automation was relegated to the realm of largely manual labor, now it has entered the world of intellectual work.[7] Again, it isn't as though these managers, administrators, and professional workers lacked for tools before. As they performed their largely information-processing-oriented tasks, they made use of communications technologies, at least since the days of telegraphs and telephones, and information technologies as rudimentary as typewriters and adding machines. It was only when this toolkit evolved, however, into modern computing technology that it seemed possible that intellectual work might be automated in the way that so much of manual labor had been.

From Efficiency to Excellence

Automation projects were first embraced with the compelling, but limited goal of *efficiency*. Using a growing set of technologies, individual workers could be made more productive. The same goods in the same quantity could be produced in far less time, at far less expense, and with far less human effort.

At a time when product and labor markets were less complex, the direct effects of this efficiency on the economics of a business—the ability to offer lower prices to customers and the chance to expand profit margins—made the justification for investment in automation simple. Soon, however, as markets evolved and enterprises grew, another enormous benefit of automation became clear. Beyond boosting the efficiency of individual workers, investments in automation equipment allowed for more *rapid scaling* of enterprises into industrial powerhouses. (See Figure 1.1.) Factory automation equipment allowed for more tightly controlled quality, greater throughput, and supply chain optimization.

Now, in a twenty-first-century economy consisting of multinational corporations operating at global scale, managers are looking to an ever-evolving set of technology options to support the creation of *business value* that encompasses more than improved efficiency and can produce scale-driven gains.

We are seeing a shift from the era of industrialized automation to a new era of intelligent automation, in which the prior focus on the costs that can be cut transitions to a new focus on the customer experience, business excellence, service improvements, innovations, and smarter strategic decisions. In other words, automation increasingly is being viewed as a way to boost top-line performance as well as bottom-line savings.

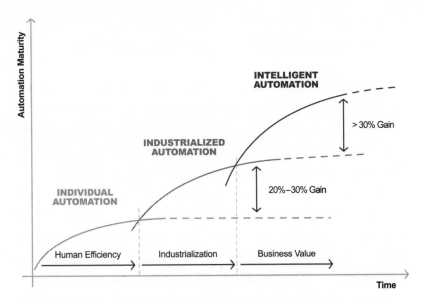

FIGURE 1.1   Conventional to Maturity Automation Journey

As part of this, we are seeing fast growth in investments in automation applications not just for back-office productivity improvements behind the scenes, but also to support the front-office work of interacting with clients and customers. This is not an either/or situation; much value generation will still come in the form of cost reduction. But the emergence of intelligent automation will also reveal many more strategically important opportunities for top-line growth and enhanced service quality. Increasingly, companies will aim beyond cost-reduction targets and use automation to enhance the customer experience, the business's ability to create value, and its revenue growth—which are all keys to remaining relevant in the future.

This new era of business value creation through automation will be marked by constant, rapid development of cognitive automation technologies. It will also be an era when managers expand their ambitions from implementing particular automation tools and solving one-off problems to establishing broad automation platforms that support and accelerate problem solving with automation throughout the business. We should expect the adoption of automation to grow exponentially as a result.

Indeed, this trend has already been established: investments in intelligent automation have increased dramatically in recent years. As reported in *Forbes*, one analyst organization predicts that the market for robotic process automation alone will add up to $12 billion by 2023.[8]

With so many companies now embarked on a transformational journey to become digital enterprises and learning fast from technology leaders, the foundations for more applications of automation in information-processing work are being laid. Combined with rapid advances in technologies related to AI, this digital revolution in business is creating endless possibilities for gaining value from machines that can sense, learn, and act.

Today, surveys find large percentages of organizations are already engaged in some form of intelligent automation. Many recognize it as a major technological breakthrough that has the potential not just to improve, but to transform the way they do business. Companies that aren't experimenting with this capability risk falling seriously behind. They need to move quickly if they hope to remain competitive.

What Is Intelligent Automation?

As discussed previously, automation has been around for many decades. By now it has been applied across a large spectrum of business functions through all kinds of technologies designed to improve performance with human-machine combinations.

What makes an application of automation *intelligent*? In simplest terms, it only means that the automation solution relies on some kind of cognitive technology, such as (but not always) AI to arrive at good decisions or recommended actions. This is a good moment to underscore that while many people tend to use the terms *AI* and *intelligent automation* interchangeably, they are not the same. An intelligent automation solution does not always need the power of natural language processing, machine learning, neural networks, or other capabilities of AI—and certainly, many applications of AI have nothing to do with automating tasks in a production environment. The two intersect when the power of AI is utilized to take in historical data, find patterns in it, and make predictions based on it.

In their most sophisticated form, intelligent automation solutions can evolve their own capabilities to recognize problems and figure out how to solve them. Just as a human mind grows more knowledgeable and capable because of its inherent capabilities to associate cause with effect and learn from that feedback, machines equipped with AI can analyze data, make decisions, observe what follows based on those decisions, and make adjustments to try to do better. Each iteration serves to further refine the algorithm and increase the intelligence level of the automation. The machines learn by generating recommendations and self-remediate over time. In some situations, it becomes possible to automate automation—to use tools to spot opportunities for better use of tools. In most situations, learning systems can adapt and improve the more they work.

We already see the impact of intelligent automation in our lives every day. Netflix provides recommendations to viewers based on AI-powered personalization algorithms. Nike, the athletic footwear, apparel, and equipment company, has developed a system that customers can use to create designs for their shoes through an augmented reality experience and leave the store wearing them.[9] Surgical robots that diagnose deadly diseases like cancer are demonstrating the impact of AI in healthcare. Across many industries, both business-to-business (B2B) and business-to-consumer (B2C), chatbots and virtual assistants are answering common customer service questions related to billing, product information, and services. Automation of these straightforward interactions proves popular with customers because it allows them to get things done at any hour, and far more quickly.

There are numerous ways in which intelligent automation is redefining possibilities and powering new levels of performance across business functions, from marketing and customer engagement to finance and accounting, and more. Smart tools—also known as intelligent systems—are being deployed to support optimized processes with sophisticated information-processing capabilities. Intelligent automation applies more and less advanced forms of automation to thoughtfully designed business processes to improve the performance of those processes— sometimes by orders of magnitude. For instance, intelligent automation can elevate the customer experience by not only managing predictable processes but also tackling more complex decisions to dramatically speed up systems and transactions.

Even without AI-level capabilities embedded in it, intelligent automation has the power to fundamentally change traditional ways of doing business, both at the operating level and at the level of individual workers and customers. These machines offer strengths (such as computational speed, accuracy, and the ability to cut through complexity) that are different from—but crucially complementary to—human skills. Rather than threatening those currently in the workplace, intelligent automation is invigorating workforces by changing the rules of what's possible. People and technology are together doing things differently— and doing different things.

The Steps to Intelligent Automation Maturity

Beyond being a set of technologies and ingenious solutions, intelligent automation should also be thought of as an organizational capability. Gaining most value from it depends on growing an organization's knowledge, skills, and other foundations.

Today, most companies have only nascent capabilities, and some have not even begun the journey toward intelligent automation. Only a small minority made investments very early and have devoted by now sufficient time and focus to grow what we would call "mature" capabilities. As always, however, the creative and experimental forays of these pioneering companies show others the possibilities and to some extent also pave pathways for them.

Our way of depicting the spectrum of organizations from least to most mature is to define five levels, reflective mainly of the *why* of their automation efforts—that is, what is driving them to invest in intelligent automation. What we have noticed is that as an enterprise matures in its capability, its managers' understanding of the opportunity they are addressing evolves. Figure 1.2 depicts this evolution as rising levels of capability, and indicates the differences involved both in the technologies applied and the sophistication of the teams implementing and using them.

This is not to imply with these stair steps that a given organization's journey has to be sequential—that a company cannot, for example, go to level four until it has gone through levels one through three. This is especially true given that companies are large, complex entities, in which different parts of the operation are often investing in automation solutions of different kinds. A back-office team, for example, might be using robotic process

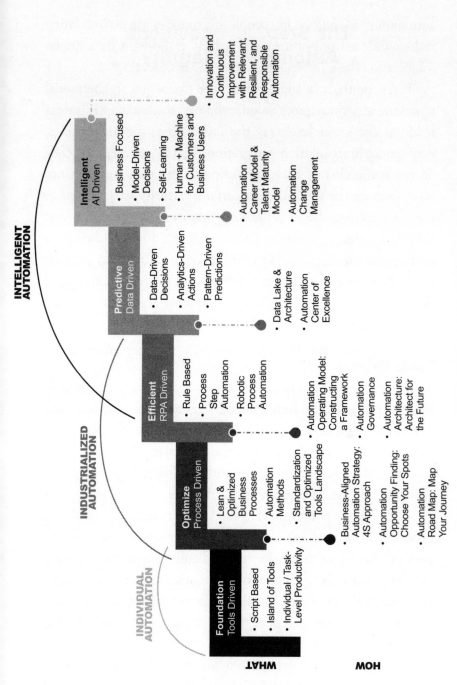

FIGURE 1.2 Automation Maturity Model

13

automation to relieve its people of routine, time-consuming tasks, while a front-office team is busy building a data-driven solution to take a service offering to the next level.

It is true that, to some extent, the five stages in the model represent a natural progression, whereby the accomplishments made at the lower levels lay the foundations for higher ones. Any automation solution integrating AI, for example, depends on the availability of data sufficient to train, test, and continuously operate the tool. Thus, a certain maturity with regard to data is a prerequisite to embarking on any AI-driven initiative. To a large extent, however, these levels are distinguished by a managerial mindset, as engagement with automation projects opens people's eyes to larger opportunities to create meaningful business impacts. Let's briefly describe what is going on at each of these five levels.

Tools Driven

At the first level of automation maturity, we see organizations intrigued by exciting, tech-enabled ways to solve perennial pain points in their businesses and by learning what it takes to implement this new class of point solutions effectively. The focus is on specific tasks—how they are currently performed by individuals and how they could be accomplished better.

Automation efforts at this level are often fragmented—as experiments, pilots, and solutions are pursued in different corners of the organization by forward-thinking teams, making choices wholly independent of each other and the tools and approaches they will use. While the kernels of a capability have been planted in the enterprise, many of these solutions will yield benefits in excess of their costs.

The overall value reaped from automation, however, will be quite limited as long as these efforts take place in pockets and do not have the benefit of learning from each other. Still, these early successes inspire more efforts and allow the people involved in them to imagine larger-scale projects with more transformative power. In terms of both skills and mindset, this level lays the foundation for a new level of automation capability.

Process Driven

In the companies we would describe as having second-level automation maturity, individuals begin to realize that a point solution has a limited impact if other parts of the process in which it is situated are not also addressed. Often, a team that has succeeded in implementing a task-focused automation solution lacks the perspective—and often lacks the authority—to take on the larger process. Only when the team's results are noted by others does the organization gain the will to take on the larger project of revisiting the process.

The narrow automation, in other words, serves to expose the inefficiency of the larger process. Of course, sometimes the results are worse than this: automation introduced without an understanding of a process's complexities can cause more issues than it solves. Companies at this level of automation maturity know that tasks exist within larger processes, and they start by reexamining the whole process, often eliminating unnecessary steps. Usually, we see them using techniques like the Lean set of principles to streamline the processes.

The Lean process improvement methodology calls for the systematic elimination of activities that add little or no value to the business. It focuses on reducing time spent on non-value-adding activities and delivering products and services right the first time. It is a customer-centric approach, continuously evaluating whether products and services are delivered at the quality, cost, and speed that business users expect. When applied to a business process, it can transform the customer experience. The Lean management philosophy aligns well with Six Sigma methodologies for quality management, and with change management leading practices. Combining these disciplines gives companies a wide range of tools to measure, analyze, and improve processes.[10]

In the banking industry, for example, process-driven automation efforts have transformed the customer experience. Gone are the days of mountains of paper-based transactions—and customers being required to physically visit bank locations to accomplish routine tasks. Now, most leading banks equip their account holders to do their banking from anywhere and on the move. The banking applications allow users to make deposits, fund transactions, stop check payments, apply for credit cards, and perform many other activities like reviewing their account balances and credit card details, all remotely.

Robotic Process Automation (RPA) Driven

The companies we see as constituting a third level of maturity in automation are those that are broadly exploiting the power of RPA. Their focus is on automating repetitive tasks that can deliver quick automation wins, but they are setting up the infrastructure and learning processes that allow one project to learn the lessons of another, and a capability to be developed at a level above the individual project.

RPA is a vendor-supplied toolkit that makes it economical for teams within an organization to automate repetitive tasks that involve interfacing with information systems—despite the fact that the teams' desire to automate this work does not rise to the level of being a priority of their internal IT organization. The robots involved are simply software programs that can easily be taught to perform a sequence of steps normally performed by an office worker to access, combine, process, and/or share information. Placing such routine tasks in the hands of the machines is not only a way to get them done faster and more accurately; the real value is that they free up the people to do less mind-numbing work.

RPA automates repetitive, rules-based processes that are predictable and involve high volumes of structured data. It emulates and integrates the actions of a human interacting within digital systems to execute a business process. Using RPA tools, a company can configure software to act autonomously, as a robot, to capture and interpret applications for processing a transaction, manipulating data, triggering responses, and communicating with other digital systems. RPA scenarios range from something as simple as generating an automatic response to an email to deploying thousands of bots, each programmed to automate jobs in an enterprise resource planning (ERP) system. An RPA software robot never sleeps and makes nearly zero mistakes.

As perhaps even this brief description makes clear, the processes that are typically automated with RPA solutions usually share several characteristics. They are routine, burdensome, high volume, and predominantly rules based. They have digital inputs, triggers, and few exceptions, and require only limited, predictable natural language interpretation. Where these conditions prevail, implementation usually is straightforward, and RPA quickly yields impressive benefits. It is not unusual to see cost reductions in the 50 to 80 percent range, as well as higher quality achieved through the avoidance of human error, and an 80 to 90 percent reduced time to perform tasks.

In many work settings, RPA-driven automation has already made everyday life easier. Thanks to RPA, paper forms are now digitized, data is inputted more quickly, claims are processed faster, and errors are rare. Popular applications include seamless onboarding of employees, streamlining the sales process by automating administrative tasks such as setting up a client in the billing system, processing most credit card applications, and more. Today's customers interact with the organization across a range of touch points and channels, from chat and interactive voice response to apps and messaging. By integrating RPA with these channels, an organization can enable its customers to do more without live interaction with human representatives.

So this is not only an investment in efficiency—the primary focus of automation since the time of its inception—but also in effectiveness. RPA often produces very quick and measurable wins, so that once it is used in one area of an organization, it spreads rapidly to others. And therefore, a key step in the typical company's automation journey is the point where management realizes that an organizational center should be established for these efforts that will build relevant knowledge of what works and save new projects from reinventing wheels. This stage lays the foundation for the journey to the higher maturity of organizations. It establishes and stabilizes a set of managerial activities that will be fundamental to pursuing data-driven and intelligent automation in bigger ways.

Data Driven

Businesses at the next major level of automation maturity exhibit much greater concern for data and how to manage it as a crucial enterprise asset. Based on what they have experienced so far, they are excited about the potential for automation to make many aspects of the business more agile and predictable, and they are acutely aware that good data is required to yield insights and intelligence. This phase lays the foundation for truly AI-driven intelligent automation and is where organizations can start to see its benefits.

Within Accenture, we have leveraged the power of data to transform many aspects of how we work. An easy example is in procurement. With offices worldwide employing more than 500,000 professionals, the company purchases a high volume of goods and services, amounting to nearly 200,000 purchase orders annually. For the global procurement organization, these amount to an average annual spend of several billion dollars, and the bills for these purchases arrive in the form of some 1.1 million invoices to be paid through the accounts payable function.

Managers realized that the processes involved in both procuring and paying could be much more optimized—in part because the individuals making buying decisions were often unfamiliar with the downstream accounting of their purchases. More generally, the processes were far from frictionless. There was ample room to take out inefficiencies and costs. In particular, the company applied intelligent automation to purchase requisitioning and non-purchase-order invoice processing by using predictive analytics and automating the recommendation of general ledger accounts to buyers at the point of purchase. Today, automated systems powered by predictive analytics equip buyers to be more accounting-savvy purchasers, and the effect downstream is a significantly streamlined accounts payable process, in terms of accuracy, time, and cost.

Most businesses today operate in more complex and dynamic environments than they did in the past. They need to balance the expectations of society, customers, and shareholders, and the tension between short-term competitive advantage and long-term sustainability. Data-driven automation can simultaneously address these challenges and help managers strike the right balance over time.

Far from being data-deprived, most organizations today are experiencing overflows of data from transactions, connected devices, and other sources. The computing power available now allows multiple algorithms to run over many disparate data sources. This means all the dots can be connected to reveal, for example, an individual customer's spend pattern and typical purchasing behavior. That analysis would also highlight preferences for certain brands or product types and enable the sending of personalized product offers to customers. This is an important way in which many businesses are leveraging the power of data to become more and more personalized and productive. Abundant data opens opportunities to connect to customers on a hyperpersonal level, capturing their attention at the right time and place with the right message.

Data-driven automation can also generate a steady stream of insights to fuel intelligent technologies. It can make faster, smarter decisions to accelerate innovation. But if an organization has only highly fragmented or low-quality data, little can be done. That kind of data cannot be mobilized. Leaders need to reimagine their organizations' data supply chains and processes to ensure transparency, trust, and accessibility. If high-quality data can be developed with all these characteristics, the return on technology and AI investments can be maximized.

Intelligence Driven

Finally, at the highest level of automation maturity, we see organizations recognizing that they can and should implement intelligent automation at scale and across the organization. Already committed to managing data as a corporate asset and having already seen the benefits of automating information-processing tasks, these are the enterprises that are most likely to be adding AI to their automation agenda.

Today, everyone's talking about AI and how it's going to forever change the way we conduct business and live our lives. Many have commented on the idea of the "fourth industrial revolution," speculating that the impact will be as great as, and potentially greater than, that of any prior technology-driven transformation. Whether or not it turns out to be the biggest technology revolution the world has ever seen, it will bring untold opportunities to reinvent individual businesses and drive revenue growth by augmenting the cognitive capabilities of human workers.

Start with the insurance industry, for example—an old and highly regulated industry. Insurance is still steeped in manual, paper-based processes that are slow and require human intervention. Even today, customers are faced with time-consuming paperwork and bureaucracy when getting a claim reimbursed or signing up for a new insurance policy. Customers may also end up paying more for insurance because policies are not tailored for their unique needs. In an age when most of our daily activities are online, digitized, and convenient, insurance is not always a happy customer experience. But today, a global push is underway by insurance companies to augment their technological capabilities so they can do business faster, cheaper, and more securely.

The past few years have seen heavy investment in AI by insurers, following decades of experience gained at lower steps of automation maturity. Most began at the level of implementing *individual tools* to perform targeted tasks more efficiently in areas such as claims management. Then they progressed to the level of *process optimization*, recognizing how advances in information technology allowed tasks to be eliminated and workflows to be accelerated. Next in their journey came *robotic process automation*, which allowed claims managers and practically any other kind of team engaged in routine information processing to hand over time-consuming task sequences to machines, freeing them up for matters requiring more judgment and creativity. At the same level, chatbots were introduced that could interact directly with customers and effectively respond to common requests— such as claims submissions or inquiries—via phone, email, or website chat feature.

At many insurers, efforts at these first three levels enforced a level of data management that made it possible to advance to *data-driven, predictive* solutions. In the claims management area, this has included automated analysis to discover fraud patterns and flag potentially fraudulent claims—an immensely valuable capability given that, according to the FBI, non-health-insurance fraud in the United States costs the industry $40 billion per year, causing the average household to pay $400 to $700 more per year in premiums.[11]

With so much automation of knowledge work accomplished already, insurers are well positioned to step up to the AI-driven solutions now possible for crafting more tailored and relevant insurance policies for individual customers and pricing them hypercompetitively. Only machines, with their vast data access and tireless processing power, can compile consumer-level offer-ings that customers recognize as including all the coverage, and only the coverage, they need—and at an attractive price. At this level of performance, not only do individual companies perform better, but the whole insurance industry prospers by appealing to a wider range of customers, including some who have never previously viewed insurance as worth the cost.

In many other industries, too, AI will take automation to astonishing new places, because it need not be limited to work that is strictly rote and rules based. It can be applied in areas that have traditionally required the human mind's ability to resolve ambiguities, deal with exceptions and novel situations, and arrive at judgment calls that balance competing priorities. That opens a huge number of new opportunities for working with machines in new ways and redirecting human talent to more rewarding work.

AI enables a business to vastly improve how it interacts with customers. In some cases, this is thanks to the power of chatbots that converse with customers at any time of the day and can help deliver uniquely personalized and trusted recommendations that create more effective and relevant e-commerce or marketing experiences. The decisions of AI are model-driven, whether it's an algorithm learning to play the highly complex board game Go better than a human; a use of computer vision to understand visual inputs with extraordinary accuracy; or predictive models that can forecast the future like never before. Machine learning and deep learning are at the heart of countless AI breakthroughs. AI enables a machine to continuously optimize its performance by learning from the success or failure of its actions.

Ethical Issues and Automation

As AI expands into areas of heightened sensitivity, such as human healthcare, it will be critical to subject the technology to greater human scrutiny.

We have seen only the beginning of the privacy intrusions, decision-making biases, and control concerns that can arise when work is performed autonomously by software and robots. Just as automation solutions are scaled up, so must be the management of ethics issues that come with them.

Any company that aims to have intelligent automation more widely applied across operations, more deeply embedded in customer solutions, and more responsible for decisions that affect lives—from medical diagnoses to government benefit payments, to mortgage approvals—must be deeply committed to the responsible automation principles presented in Chapter 9.

Too many AI applications today are effectively black boxes lacking the ability to explain the reasoning behind their decisions. As humans and machines work together even more, effective explanations will be at the very heart of this collaboration. The future of AI lies in enabling people to collaborate with machines to solve complex problems. Like any efficient collaboration, this requires good communication, trust, and understanding. Deploying AI now involves more than training it to perform a given task. It's about "raising" it to act as a responsible representative of the business.

In their recent book, *Human + Machine: Reimagining Work in the Age of AI*, Paul Daugherty and Jim Wilson show that as humans and smart machines collaborate ever more closely, work processes become more fluid and adaptive, enabling companies to change them on the fly—or to completely reimagine them. As we look around, we see the journey to AI underway in every industry—and it's picking up pace. The result of this rapid, broad-based adoption is that intelligent automation isn't an option any longer. It is mandatory. The question is whether an organization has the capabilities to implement it across every aspect of its operations—and to reap the full benefits.

Fashion Designer Gives Wings to Designers' Imaginations

One of the world's fastest-growing fashion companies built an AI application capable of breaking down its product offerings into their various elements and then recombining those elements to suggest and design new concepts more heavily weighted toward attributes trending in popularity. This gives wings to designers' imaginations, combining their creative art with the science of tracking trending products. Specifically, the development team leveraged AI techniques to help designers:

- **Analyze dress attributes and understand the market trends.** The AI application is trained to identify the key elements of a dress and predict future consumer inclination from sales and margin data.
- **Create new apparel designs by recombining concepts from existing trending apparel.** The algorithm takes the attributes of the most trending styles and generates new designs leveraging enhanced AI techniques such as deep neural networks.
- **Create digital variants with various colors.** The AI algorithm generates different color variants of apparel using a style transfer approach.
- **Create digital variants by applying trending patterns.** Trending patterns are identified using trendspotting algorithms and transferred to the apparel using the trained AI models.

The same concept can be used across industries. Expect to see such applications take hold in hospitality, home furnishing, advertising, fashion, and more.

Key Takeaways

- ▶ Intelligent automation is a form of automation that brings higher performance to information-based work—not only by increasing its cost efficiency but by elevating the customer experience and boosting top-line growth.
- ▶ Every company is currently at some stage of maturity regarding intelligent automation—and some are building that capability into a core competence, to be applied throughout the business.
- ▶ Unlike past investments in automation, today's must be "people first" in their orientation, designed to leverage human strengths and supported by investments in skills, experience, organization, and culture.

Beware the Barriers

I n most large organizations, the argument for investing more in intelligent automation is easy to make.

Intelligent automation can be applied to achieve higher levels of performance in numerous areas, spanning departments, geographies, and initiatives. Managers we talk with see possibilities for using it at every level of the business, from streamlining accounts payable to personalizing customer service to identifying acquisition opportunities. In a recent Accenture survey, 84 percent of business executives expressed the belief that their organizations would need to apply AI in their operations to achieve their growth objectives.[1]

In that case, why isn't intelligent automation already more pervasive than it is? What's holding companies back? In the same survey, over three-quarters of respondents reported facing barriers to automation and AI application. Fully 76 percent acknowledged struggling with how to scale intelligent automation across their business.[2] For some, organizational structures got in the way, for others the worst problems had to do with data, and still others cited reluctance by employees to adopt the new tools. As with most capabilities promising the chance of great leaps forward, there are stumbling blocks.

A simple shorthand that management thinkers have long used to talk about the major elements that have to be considered in any substantial change initiative—people, process, technology, and strategy—applies equally well to examining where challenges most commonly arise in intelligent automation. This chapter looks within these categories to explore the biggest roadblocks getting in the way of some organizations' journeys. It also, however, exposes some *pseudo*-barriers—that is, misconceptions and knowledge gaps that get in the way of success even though they shouldn't. These are the myths of intelligent automation that cause hesitancy, false starts, or complacency. They are, in their own way, some of the biggest obstacles to be removed.

Barrier 1:
A Shortage of Talent and Skills

Any company that intends to invest meaningfully in intelligent automation needs a diversely talented and reconfigured workforce to support and scale it. In survey after survey, business managers identify workforce issues as their greatest barrier: intelligent automation skills are in short supply, and therefore hard to find and expensive to hire.[3]

Across industries from insurance to education and across functional areas from IT to HR, hiring managers looking for developers, business analysts, program managers, and project managers are putting a premium on intelligent automation skill sets and driving salaries upward. Take the extreme case of a top-notch AI researcher. Peter Lee, a vice president inside Microsoft

Research, once said that acquiring this level of talent is as challenging and expensive as acquiring a star quarterback in the National Football League.[4]

Short of that stratospheric level, companies are often more than willing to pay for talent, but they struggle to find it. In an O'Reilly AI Adoption in the Enterprise 2021 survey, respondents cited lack of skilled people and difficulty in hiring as the number one bottleneck to AI adoption, reinforcing the ongoing talent gap.[5]

Despite the shortage of AI talent, the commitment for retraining to develop AI skills internally does not appear as strong as what is needed. A 2018 Accenture study of 1,200 CEOs and top executives working with AI showed that even though almost half of business leaders identified skills shortages as a key workforce challenge, only 3 percent said their organization planned to increase investment in training programs significantly in the next three years.[6]

What kinds of skills are we talking about? Organizations need both the skills to develop AI and automation solutions and the skills to use them effectively. Clearly, a wide variety of talents go into the design, implementation, and scaling of intelligent automation solutions. Key competencies needed for automation engineers include skills in automation analysis, programming, software development, data analytics, data visualization, and IT security—on top of a firm grounding in ethics. In addition, organizations need expertise in the advanced technologies involved, such as robotic process automation, voice recognition, natural language processing, machine learning, and other forms of AI.

Moreover, at the team level, it can be a struggle to combine just the right mix of talent—in addition to the relevant technical skills. Teams should be interdisciplinary from the start, bringing together industry, business, design, and governance expertise in the right degrees. Some of these areas of knowledge might seem like nice-to-haves, but they all play crucial roles in giving a company an automation edge.

Meanwhile, on the receiving end of intelligent automation tools, there may also be important knowledge and skills deficits to address. Inevitably, automation affects job structures as it identifies the work that machines can handle and where human labor for oftentimes tedious tasks can be eliminated. Especially for workers in low- and middle-skilled roles, this may lead to significant job redesign, requiring some uplift of skills.

In some cases, the content of work will change to such an extent that typical education and training practices will not be sufficient. All automating organizations should be thinking, however, of how to develop the capabilities of the employees who will apply these new tools in their work, so they can both use them effectively and take advantage of freed-up time to add value in new ways. Successful implementation of sophisticated automation requires people to adjust to new ways of working.

Barrier 2:
Organizational Resistance

If skills deficits are one side of the people barriers to intelligent automation, then the other side is made up of the organizational cultural challenges that can develop and hinder a company's efforts. Often, initiatives run up against long-established habits, attitudes, and assumptions that make it hard for change to take hold, whether due to deliberate defiance or simple apathy—or just because everyone is running flat out with today's workload and can't spare the mental energy required to do things differently.

Low Cultural Flexibility

When Avanade conducted a recent survey about AI maturity, 80 percent of respondents agreed that business culture and change are the make-or-break items for AI's long-term success.[7]

In a sense, change resistance is a larger barrier than any skills shortage. People who are eager to embrace a new way of working are often quick to learn whatever new approaches are needed, even without formal instruction. People who, on the other hand, lack any enthusiasm about a proposed change can manage to remain unaffected by even the most wonderful teaching methods.

Sometimes, as discussed in the following section, resistance is the result of workers feeling directly threatened by new technology. Other times, their lack of enthusiasm reflects skepticism about the value of the change, and a sense that precious time is being wasted on an experiment that will end up going nowhere. Perhaps most common of all, resistance is rooted in simple inertia. People have learned to get things done in a certain way, and as far as they are concerned, that process is working well enough as is.

As discussed more in Chapter 7, change resistance doesn't always take the form of conscious pushback—and it should never be seen as insurmountable. None of the barriers discussed in this chapter are. But like all the others, it can derail an intelligent automation initiative if it is not recognized and responded to as a barrier. Just as in the case of skills deficits, change resistance has to be acknowledged where it exists and deliberately addressed.

Fears of Job Destruction

To be sure, there is plenty of uncertainty about intelligent automation in today's workplaces, if not downright fear of what it means for the future of work. Millions of words have already been published about how the rise of AI and automation could destroy whole categories of jobs and leave even highly educated knowledge workers with no higher ground to move to. According to *CIO Insight,* 60 percent of people surveyed specifically about the prospect of their organizations applying intelligent automation believe workers will lose their jobs as a result. No wonder that the same survey finds 72 percent of respondents at the C-suite level saying the adoption of advanced technologies has been limited by employee resistance and unreadiness.[8]

It's true that intelligent automation has the potential to seriously disrupt labor, and it is already doing just that. Some traditional jobs will become obsolete. Seeing this, however, as a straightforward transfer of labor from humans to machines is a vast oversimplification. There's very little factual evidence to suggest that mass unemployment or widespread redundancy of human workforces will result from growing automation. In fact, it is just as possible that a more productive economy, brought about by the increased efficiency and reduction of waste that automation promises, will provide workers with more attractive options for engaging in value-generating and well-compensated pursuits.

Employers are generally looking at cognitive technologies as a means of augmenting the highest-value strengths of their human workforces and enabling their people to work more safely, more creatively, and more empathically. This opens up opportunities for businesses to leverage employee talents for more strategic and transformational programs. Successful enterprises have always tagged and aligned their automation transformation programs with the business transformation agendas so as to accelerate the creation of value.

Barrier 3:
Subpar Processes and Outdated Policies

Process problems can appear in two fundamental ways in intelligent automation efforts. First, the processes and policies being subjected to automation can be suboptimal, poorly defined and implemented, or interconnected with other business processes in ways that are not well understood. Second, the project management processes being used by the automation team itself can be flawed.

Suboptimal Work Processes

In the first category, the biggest of these problems is the surprise that confronts many teams as they embark on what would seem to be straightforward automation projects. As they get down to the work of identifying the parts of a workflow that could be handed off from people to machines, they map out all its steps at a detailed level. That's when it often comes to light that the process was not well designed at the start. It might have been optimized at some point in the past, but not revisited as steps within it changed or new technologies were introduced. More likely, it was never optimized, but was simply a way of doing things that people tried and, once satisfied, adopted it as a standard operating procedure. People continued to follow those steps and, perhaps with some workarounds and exception management, got good enough results. But it is far from the most efficient or foolproof process to accomplish its goal.

Veteran managers all know this time-honored principle: don't automate a bad process, or you'll only succeed at taking the wrong steps faster. Sometimes it's best to begin with a clean slate and redesign the process in light of current reality.

Let's say some long-established process calls for three approvals. Is that really necessary, or would two approvals suffice?

Sometimes it's helpful to look at a process from the perspective of its customer rather than its contributors. Are their attempts to interface with it more time-consuming or convoluted than they need to be? Could some steps be combined to streamline the process and improve the customer experience?

The point is process doesn't have to be a barrier to success in intelligent automation if an organization pauses to get it right before automating parts of its operations.

Outdated Policies

Sometimes the barrier that trips up an automation solution the worst is never considered by the team because it isn't strictly in the scope of their creative problem-solving work: it's a corporate policy or set of policies that as written throws up a brick wall to implementing an essential part of the new approach.

Experienced automation leaders know that their project plans must explicitly include a timely review of corporate policies related to the solution design. And they understand and anticipate that time and effort may have to go into modifying policies that conflict with the project. Typically, this is not as politically difficult as it may sound, because many policies are easily proven to be antiquated or designed to address old issues or old processes that no longer apply. On the other hand, many legal, financial, and human resource policies are in place for very good reasons and remain immovable. Coming to grips and adjusting for those realities early on can be critical to an automation team's success.

Poorly Defined and Implemented Processes

Attempts to automate an underlying process can also run into complications if the automation approach is opaque. This is the case when a process is basically sound, but there is little accurate documentation or transparency around it. It is difficult to proceed without knowing all the steps—the tasks, sequences, and actions that the process comprises. As we think about it, it strikes us this is why intelligent automation has taken hold so quickly in certain areas of IT, operations, production, and finance. They follow well-known, easily mapped sequences.

Take an IT process like password management, for example, or logging of service requests. The steps are unambiguous. The same goes for a process like maintenance scheduling in operations, or the tasks involved in invoicing and accounts payable in a typical finance department. Compared to these clearly specified processes, many other business processes feature more ambiguity and variety. Before they can be appropriately automated, they need to be similarly well defined and understood.

Confusing Interconnectivity

Similarly, the fact that various processes in a business interact in complex ways can present a barrier to intelligent automation. Few processes exist in such isolation that they can be carved out, retooled substantially with new technologies, and then expected to still interface seamlessly with upstream and downstream workflows. Managers hoping to apply automation to their groups' work may need to negotiate with other process owners less interested in making adjustments.

Even where a process can be redesigned on its own for greater efficiency, it may not produce much impact if other processes are left as they are. Consider an insurance company applying intelligent automation to speed up the work of drafting an individual customer's policy. That might not have any effect on the customer experience if the separate process of customer approval is not also accelerated.

The Process of Automation Itself

All these barriers have to do with the process that is the target of automation, but it's important to note that automating work is a process in itself that can be more or less well mapped out and managed. When it comes to how companies go about developing and rolling out their intelligent automation solutions, most are held back to some extent by outdated processes for managing automation projects. This, of course, is a major topic of this book and the main barrier we and our colleagues help clients to overcome. Chapter 4 returns to the subject.

Barrier 4:
A Technology Environment
Built for a Previous Era

Technology barriers can seem like the least of an organization's worries with regard to intelligent automation. With machine learning and other AI tools rapidly advancing, sensors proliferating, and computing power growing steadily, new hardware and software tools are finding their way into practical applications across virtually every sector of the global economy. Huge and growing numbers of solutions are already available from vendors, and many of them are producing impressive results. Yet most companies encounter barriers as they try to make use of these technologies. The barriers show up in the form of legacy architectures, inadequate data, and off-the-shelf solutions that are not nearly as turnkey as their vendors can make them seem.

Legacy Architectures

First, there is the enormous challenge of innovating with legacy systems. The typical organization's IT stack—spanning software applications, data, hardware, telecommunications, facilities, and data centers—was built for an earlier age, when none of the people laying those foundations could envision a cloud-oriented world of analytics, sensors, mobile computing, AI, the Internet of Things (IoT), and billions and billions of devices. That is the world that exists today—and we should fully expect a new wave of revolutionary changes to reshape it into a different world of tomorrow.

A legacy architecture constitutes a barrier when it makes it hard to bring in new applications or make enhancements to applications built on that old foundation. It is important to note that most companies' enterprise architectures were not only based on different technological foundations; they also were built on a presumption that the functions they supported would be stable and enduring. They did not anticipate the constant introduction of new applications that is the reality of most companies today.

Every new application raises the same question: What dependencies exist between the application being introduced and other applications also on that architecture? There might be 25 other applications that must be taken into consideration before work can begin in earnest on the one new solution that was envisioned. Say, for example, that an online retailer becomes aware of a new payment option and wants to make it available to its customers—perhaps a hot new mobile app is gaining in popularity, and a retailer risks losing sales if it cannot include that new option in its ordering process. To add that new payment option on the legacy architecture, the retailer would have to first assess what impact it would have elsewhere in that architecture.

This is not a new problem; the barrier presented by legacy systems has always meant that there is a high bar for a new solution to be considered worth doing. It grows successively worse, however, every time a company adds a new application. Each successive generation of additions brings more complexity as old interconnections are disrupted and new ones are created.

By now, the conventional IT stack has truly reached its practical limit. Until a business goes to the very substantial effort of redefining both its business and IT architectures, it will have to deal with barriers as it tries to integrate the advanced tools of AI. Indeed, given the revolutionary potential of AI, these new architectures should be AI-centric—constructed at every layer in ways that place top priority on supporting it.

As we enter the 2020s, many companies' IT leaders would describe the barrier they face as a lack of a *microservices architecture*. This very modern style of architecture enables greater flexibility by decoupling data, infrastructure, and applications—three elements that in traditional software solutions are bundled together. Think of this as an architecture consisting of boxes—small groupings of applications that are as independent as possible, so that making a change to one of them will have minimal ramifications downstream or elsewhere in the system. Now, picture the opposite: hundreds of applications with their links impossibly tangled together, their interconnections having been complicated by generation after generation of applications. That is the picture of today's barriers in most organizations; it presents a nearly impenetrable thicket against new automation applications.

Inadequate Data

Another foundational barrier for most companies is the state of their data. This is a barrier particular to intelligent automation because especially where machine-learning algorithms are deployed, the systems require data in prodigious volumes.

Few companies complain that they have too little data; today's digital mechanisms for information gathering and processing produce a tsunami of data points. The problem is that too little of it is usable, either because of poor quality or because of limited accessibility. Often there are difficulties in integrating data stored in different formats. This is exacerbated when mergers and acquisitions result in separate pools of data that should be combined but aren't. One recent study estimated that 97 percent of a typical company's decisions are made using data that its own managers think is of unacceptable quality.[9]

The way to think about this barrier productively is to see it not as a lack of adequate data but as a lack of good data management strategy. Usually, the data exists in some form for companies to produce real-time insights and actions, but it remains locked in unstructured and semistructured forms. It has to be cleansed, engineered, and optimized to be useful to decision-making and automated action. One bright spot is that automation itself can help. So-called capture software, for example, now exists to automate data capture in currently unfriendly forms and to do the content analysis, identification of key elements, and extraction required to make it useful for an enterprise's business systems and applications.

Disappointment with Turnkey Solutions

The number of vendor solutions available in the realm of intelligent automation has exploded in recent years. Just look at the startup space. Entrepreneurial activity and funding of new companies is so high that the annual list produced by *CB Insights* of just the fraction of AI startups that are "most promising" includes a hundred new companies each year.[10]

It might seem like the only barrier is an embarrassment of riches from which to choose. But it's important to understand that these solutions do not have the generic level of functionality that IT departments usually get from off-the-shelf enterprise software. In particular, to the extent that the software needs to be trained on a specific company's data, it is not reasonable to expect a plug-and-play solution from a vendor. A lot of work still has to go into making it work in the company's own environment.

The fact that vendor solutions typically don't work right out of the box presents a barrier that sometimes surprises company managers eager to make progress with intelligent automation. Worse, it may cause them to gravitate toward only those small-scale point solutions that can be used without much tailoring or training. In that case, they may face different kinds of barriers: not being able to scale the solutions and failing to think holistically about what would help the business achieve its most strategic goals.

Barrier 5: Lack of Strategic Alignment

When intelligent automation is managed most strategically, the thinking happens on two levels. First, there is a clear plan for building an intelligent automation capability within the organization, stating its major goals in clear terms and outlining an action plan well designed to achieve them. Second, there is alignment of the intelligent automation solutions pursued with the overall business strategy. Writing in *MIT Sloan Management Review*, David Kiron and Michael Schrage refer to this pair of strategic perspectives as having a "strategy *for and with* AI."[11] Insufficient attention to either of these levels is a barrier to success.

Unclear Goals

A common strategic barrier in intelligent automation efforts arises where managers have not taken the time to specify their goals in objectively measurable terms, based on current baseline performance numbers. If a specific project aims, for example, to enhance the performance of a call center, it is not enough to state a goal like "we will automate the process of opening case numbers." The project needs to specify, for example, that it aims to reduce handling errors by 40 percent and cut processing time by 80 percent. Implied here is that the team would have an accurate awareness of today's handling error rates and average processing time. These become the key metrics by which the project's progress (and ultimate success) will be gauged.

Unclear Metrics

A lack of salient metrics becomes a barrier to future automation because it leaves intelligent automation proponents unable to point to proven benefits. But it also presents barriers to the effective management of the current automation project, as the team lacks the clear targets it needs to keep its efforts on track.

At the outset of an automation effort, a team should spell out the end value it hopes to realize, in whatever forms that value will take. Cost savings are often targeted most prominently, in part because they are easier to measure and can be used to show a project's return on investment. But intelligent automation can also be applied to increase speed or enhance quality, perhaps by simplifying a process or by giving time back to customers. Often, improvements along these two lines have far more impact than incremental cost savings to a company's competitive advantage, growth, and long-term success. It is vital not only to establish clear metrics, but also to measure what really matters.

No Road Map or Strategic Plan

Along with clear goals, a strategy for automation needs to spell out how the team will achieve those goals over a planned time horizon. A major barrier to high-impact success in most companies is the lack of such a road map. Many have not developed this disciplined way of managing initiatives because their adoption and implementation of automation, analytics, and AI has so far been done in piecemeal fashion—in a spirit of experimentation and in pockets of the organization that happened to have high interest and sufficient skill. Without a structured road map, however, they cannot progress as fast or as effectively as they could.

Any project needs its own road map, but at the highest level, a company's overall road map should represent its resolve to realize the full potential of intelligent automation. It should map the journey from its current automation starting point to an automation destination at which business goals are routinely being set and met across the business by employees augmented in creative ways by transformative automation technologies.

As Chapter 4 discusses much more, an intelligent automation road map is essentially the strategy for how automation will be developed and introduced for greatest cumulative impact. Companies that lack this road map are held back by a patchwork of ways of working and fail to take on the challenge of updating systems that were built for the business needs of years ago. The older technologies they depend on are not up to the challenge of meeting tomorrow's business goals.

No Sound Basis for Prioritizing Projects

We just discussed how intelligent automation should be approached as a structured journey, with a "you are here" road map to simplify this step and help teams determine how to proceed. That journey, moreover, is not just a journey of enterprise technology deployment. It is a voyage of transformation at the level of the business model and certainly the operating model. As Kiron and Schrage insist, having a "strategy *for* AI is not enough. Creating strategy *with* AI matters as much—or even more—in terms of exploring and exploiting strategic opportunity."

The worst strategic blunder is the one that has plagued IT departments since they were first established: a lack of alignment between their projects and the priorities of the business. Without such alignment, intelligent automation projects often lack a clear business case. A surprising proportion of organizations are hobbled right out of the gate because they have not made a compelling case for how intelligent automation will lead to competitive advantage in the marketplace.[12] Thus, they lack a defensible position on precisely what they should automate and in what order, and struggle to persuade leadership to commit to an intelligent automation program at meaningful scale.

Making strategic choices requires having a way to prioritize, but a big barrier for many companies is the lack of an *opportunity assessment process*. This results in a situation that might be described as "a thousand initiatives blooming." We recently visited a multinational business that had more than 300 separate automation initiatives in play—yet none of them were connected. Leaders were approaching automation on an ad hoc basis, adopting tools to solve problems identified by particular teams, and for the most part picking low-hanging fruit. Some technology-driven organizations with hundreds of technology options have many trials happening simultaneously. Other enterprises take a fragmented approach to applying automation—identifying opportunities à la carte and implementing discrete tools to solve isolated problems.

We see some companies automating prolifically—but targeting the wrong things. Should the priority be a global operations and supply chain solution? Perhaps an inventory management process? A fix for training and development gaps? It is possible for intelligent automation to add tangible value to almost any process or decision by dialing in speed, efficiency, problem solving, and adaptability. Yet enterprise capacity for change is limited in any given time frame. Strategic choices have to be made. A company must have a process of sorting the opportunities into categories such as quick hits, strategically important advantages, and so forth.

To be sure, there can be good reasons for starting small, proceeding with caution, and launching experiments. It is typical for a company to simply look for repetitive tasks to automate, on the assumption that the financial benefit will materialize. But if efforts are too siloed, the synergies that could be exploited enterprisewide are being lost. Pursuing automation in disconnected silos limits the power and enterprisewide efficiency that automation could deliver. A lot of companies get stalled in pilot phase or early-stage AI adoption. The problem is that they are implementing the technology in silos and discrete projects. This approach not only lacks an enterprise-level view, but it also introduces increasing layers of complexity and thwarts scalability.

At worst, it means that resources are being spent on automation efforts that don't ultimately benefit the business much at all. Take the example of deploying a virtual agent to automate some standard reporting. Automation of reporting is a very common wish-list item for managers because it seems obvious: reporting is tedious work and so rule-based that it is absolutely conducive to automation. And yet, what is the impact for the business to have that activity automated? Certainly, it saves some portion of an employee's time, but usually that doesn't amount to much, and if that is the sum total of the value it delivers, the impact on the business is minimal.

By contrast, imagine if the virtual agent had been deployed to detect and issue alerts about something mission critical—perhaps informing engineers that an outage was imminent that would mean the company would incur serious downtime in a core area. Compared to this, the use of a virtual agent to save some back-office reporting labor is a waste. There is always a tendency to get excited about a tool and see use cases for it—but some things are not worth the investment.

Four Myths of Intelligent Automation

The barriers discussed previously are all very real, but companies can also be held back by barriers that are only perceived to exist. Call them myths (or mindset barriers)—flawed ideas that keep people from seeing opportunities and acting on them. In a sense, much of this book will be devoted to myth-busting. At the outset, here are a few big ones to dispel.

Myth 1: Our Customers Aren't Ready for It

The point of intelligent automation is to enable a company's scarcest and hardest-to-scale assets—its talented people—to focus on only those tasks that machines cannot do. Strengths in human qualities and abilities such as leadership, creativity, persuasiveness, critical thinking, and intuition will remain the source of the company's competitive edge, precisely *because* they are hard to replicate. Talented people will gravitate to organizations with human qualities: building personal relationships, managing employee concerns, helping managers solve pressing problems, and improving employee engagement and satisfaction.

To be sure, there are data privacy and security concerns among customers (and those protecting their interests), especially in public sector and healthcare organizations. No company should ignore these. But neither should any company resist automating based on an unfounded belief that people will only interface with people.

Myth 2: Succeeding with Intelligent Automation Is Overwhelmingly a Technology Challenge

There is a widespread misconception that in the era of intelligent automation the way to prevail is by winning the technology arms race. According to this thinking, technologies are the critical source of competitive advantage—and the organization that is best at scouting the leading edge and in the best position to buy the newest and most expensive tools will come out on top.

The reality is that winning with intelligent automation is about making it work for people. Again, the point of intelligent automation is to leverage workers' talents. This means that succeeding with intelligent automation is at least as much a challenge of understanding people's needs, introducing new technologies in a way that is helpful and involves minimal disruption, and addressing any needs for new skills, roles, and job content. It is, in other words, mainly a people challenge.

Myth 3: It's Best Not to Be a Pioneer

Perhaps another way of phrasing this myth would be to say: It's folly to jump in when technologies are evolving so fast. Why not wait for the dust to settle, let others take the risks of implementing tools on the "bleeding edge," and fast follow when it becomes clearer which of these technologies is paying off best?

It's true that the blistering pace of innovation in this field has a serious downside. On some level, whatever is put in place will quickly become obsolete. In a 2019 Accenture survey of more than 6,600 business and IT executives, 94 percent of respondents said the pace of technology innovation in their organizations had either accelerated or significantly accelerated over the past three years.[13] This can make it seem like it's never the right moment to jump in. In Accenture's enterprise systems survey, however, the respondents who expressed more faith in a fast-follower approach tended strongly to be in the "laggards" category, who were underperforming in general in their use of automation. Only 42 percent of the laggards, for example, had yet made any investment in growing their AI toolkit.

The reality is that it's folly to sit on the sidelines while others achieve and learn. The Economist Intelligence Unit 2019 survey of 502 executives across eight countries finds 73 percent of them claiming to be either "very" or "entirely satisfied" with the automation benefits they are seeing.[14]

This indicates that the risks of jumping into the fray now are not as great as some managers might imagine. Yes, the toolkit will continue to evolve rapidly. Yes, there will be some regrets about having headed down what turned out to be blind alleys. But the bigger problem is losing out on the learning dividends of working with viable technologies today. Those using intelligent automation will be able to set new standards of not only speed and efficiency but also quality and functionality. Companies that successfully apply intelligent automation will beat competitors that do not.

Myth 4: Once a Process Has Been Automated, We're Done and Can Stop Thinking About It

Fire up Google and type in "what to automate" in a specific industry or functional area. It will promptly serve up lists of the usual suspects for intelligent automation. If your search specified the insurance sector, for example, you'll learn that the usual starting point is x, y, and z. Most companies in that sector either have automation in place in those areas or are working under great pressure now to put it in place. Given the pressure, it's tempting to take a "check the box" mindset, taking satisfaction in the processes that are already "done" and focusing on different processes to take on next.

The reality is that automation is iterative and ongoing. After automating a task or process, a company needs to keep making step-change improvements, especially by combining robotic process automation, AI, and modern engineering.

Say, for example, that a bank has successfully applied robotic process automation to allow customers to check their credit card balances. Now, instead of having to call during office hours or waiting in a call center queue to talk to a human agent, they have the convenience of a chatbot interface to answer their question. The key for the bank is not to say "mission accomplished" at that point. But what about taking that chatbot and converting it later into a virtual/conversational agent, which then begins to know the source of the query as a customer? How could it do more with that customer touchpoint than simply spitting out the answer the customer directly queried it about? There are always new opportunities and further steps that can be added to a basic solution once it is up and running. The automation journey need never be done.

▲ ▲ ▲

This chapter touched on the many barriers that get in the way of intelligent automation even as enterprises of all sizes recognize its great potential. We've organized them into the convenient and familiar management framework of people, process, strategy, and technology. While the tone has been cautionary—as any discussion focused on barriers must be—the real message we want readers to take away from the chapter is an optimistic one: all these barriers are surmountable.

Managers just need a full awareness of the barriers, and a structured way to tackle and overcome them. Chapter 3 starts with a discussion of the strategic challenge of intelligent auto-mation and how to build a case for investment based on the priorities of the business.

Key Takeaways

▸ There are very real barriers to overcome in applying intelligent automation, relating to people, process, technology, and strategy. This book focuses on helping organizations overcome them.

▸ But many efforts are also held back by myths: that customers aren't ready for automation, that intelligent automation solutions are mainly technology projects, that "fast following" is safer than being a pioneer, and that once a solution is put in place, it requires no more managerial attention.

▸ For their organizations to thrive in the era of intelligent automation, leaders must recognize the barriers, reject the myths, and design the initiatives that can move beyond them.

Start with Strategic Intent

There are many examples today of enterprises evolving their business strategy and, in some cases, turning it upside down to remain competitive and lead their industries.

This is certainly true in telecommunications. One telecommunications company we know has approached intelligent automation very strategically. Given the pace of innovation it wants to sustain in introducing a steady stream of new pricing strategies, subscriber benefits, and promotions—and the level of efficiency it has to achieve as its rivals quickly follow suit with their own similar packages and promotions—effective strategic planning is an absolute necessity.

Like most companies, it used what is known as a waterfall methodology for developing new software solutions. It started out each fiscal year by specifying and allocating the budget to a set plan of initiatives. If the company wanted to bring a next wave of innovations to market featuring, say, 15 projects, it would plan out all 15 of them at the beginning of the year and map out extended timelines showing when clean hand-offs would occur from the software developers to the testers to the people managing broad deployment. Several years ago, the company recognized that this approach was hindering it from acting quickly on ideas and opportunities—and that even when a project was undertaken, it was taking longer than it should for software to be deployed and for customers to start reaping the benefits.

What followed was a large-scale transformation to make two changes in the software development process: first, it moved away from waterfall and other traditional methodologies and instead embraced the new approaches known as Agile and DevOps, and second, it applied intelligent automation to the process from end to end. This made development less costly, but even more important, it made it faster and surer.

Automating many parts of the development and testing process, for example, gave the company a much better gauge of release readiness. With this better ability to predict performance after rollout, it is experiencing a greater success rate on the releases it brings to market. Meanwhile, thanks to the collapsing of timelines possible with Agile and DevOps, the company is also bringing new releases to market at eight times the rate it did in the past. Innovation has become so frequent and fluid that managers talk about having an approach that treats adaptation as a constant growth process rather than a disruptive event.

What can this company's experience teach others about succeeding with intelligent automation? A big part of its approach is that it thinks strategically about automation on three levels: applying it in the ways that will best advance the business strategy; devising smart strategies for building IT systems capabilities; and setting ambitious and clearly articulated goals for particular solutions. The companies we see getting the most from their intelligent automation investments are thoughtful about their strategies on all these levels. The sections that follow explore each of them in turn.

Automation Aligned with Business Strategy

Everything begins with achieving clarity about the strategy of the business and aligning information technology to support the strategy. In a view that was developed more than 30 years ago and is still relevant today, strategy experts Gary Hamel and C. K. Prahalad coined the term *strategic intent* after looking for the common keys to success in a set of companies that had risen to global leadership in the preceding two decades.[1] Invariably, they found leading companies could state the single most important goal they were trying to achieve. "Strategic intent envisions a desired leadership position and establishes the criterion the organization will use to chart its progress," they wrote.

When a management team articulates the strategic intent of an enterprise, it is making a compelling, succinct statement about where that enterprise is going and what it wants to achieve in the long term. It isn't enough to have a mission statement. While the mission of an organization is meant to endure, strategy constantly adapts in response to the business environment to say how that mission will be achieved.

Hamel and Prahalad also found, in the thriving companies they studied, that leaders had made exceptional efforts to translate their ambitions into actionable directions. The concept of strategic intent, they stressed, "also encompasses an active management process that includes focusing the organization's attention on the essence of winning, motivating people by communicating the value of the target, leaving room for individual and team contributions, sustaining enthusiasm by providing new operational definitions as circumstances change, and using intent consistently to guide resource allocations."

Automation is one of the many areas in which team contributions and resource allocations should be guided by strategic intent—rather than being made in a haphazard, isolated, or ill-informed fashion. Intelligent automation efforts should be managed from the outset with an eye to how they can advance the intended competitive advantage, even to the level of enabling business model transformation. Is your company, for example, intending to compete on price and focusing relentlessly on market-share gains? Or is the intent to out-innovate competitors and command higher margins? Competing proposals for automation projects have to be prioritized in terms of how much they support the business along the strategic path it is trying to pursue.

A key point to underscore here is that intelligent automation can be integral to pursuing any strategic intent. It is not only a means to reduce costs, time, and errors—which is the typical way in which managers think about automation. Intelligent automation is just as crucial to advancing business strategies that call for developing other capabilities—for example, personalized customer service, accelerated business scaling, more informed decision-making, or better risk, security, and compliance management.

The companies getting the most from their automation investments choose their projects with more of an eye to strategic and long-term payoffs that really matter and applications that provide an automation edge. This is why business leaders must cocreate the intelligent automation strategy with IT leaders. The business unit needs to own the outcomes to be delivered, and be thoroughly prepared to participate in the ongoing monitoring, adjustment, and new creation of the intelligent automation capabilities. Only if business-side managers are energized by the strategy up front, will they dedicate the people necessary to support the execution and sustain the gains.

At the telecommunications company we talked about earlier, the goal was to grow the customer base by out-innovating competitors. Elsewhere, the objective might be to enrich customer interactions and relationships. At luxury fashion retailer Moda Operandi, for example, high-touch service is an imperative, as customers expect personalized recommendations from stylists and one-to-one communications that show they are understood and valued.[2] How does that translate to any kind of automation opportunity? Some high-end merchants would assume not at all or only in functions of the business that clients don't see or interact with.

Moda Operandi understood things differently. Recognizing that the biggest constraint on a traditional fashion retailer's growth was the difficulty of finding stylists with top-notch fashion taste, social graces, and organizational skills, it actively sought ways to leverage that crucial talent with intelligent systems. As the company's chief technology officer, Keiron McCammon, explained, Moda Operandi collected behavioral data from various sources and "developed in-house algorithms leveraging machine learning to recommend products to stylists based on client behavior, who then hand-curate look books for their clients."[3] Thanks to this new personalization engine, a stylist who in the past could have consulted to perhaps 50 or 75 clients can now provide the same valuable attention to up to 300. Luxury service is no longer limited to a tiny percentage of fashionistas.

Often, new technologies create the reason and the need to refresh business strategies, as companies find themselves competing under new conditions, against more agile organizations. In the banking industry, for example, the march of technology has forced many strategic transformations over the decades. Today, any bank that does not offer its customers an app capable of dispensing personalized financial advice and pathways to achieving financial goals is at a serious competitive disadvantage. But these systems—which effortlessly monitor incoming funds, patterns of expenditure, and personal spending habits to produce their suggestions—have depended on advances in analytics and AI to power them. Likewise, today's convenient reminders to pay bills and invitations to learn more about financial issues and services became possible only with the rise of smart devices and mobile apps.

What might come next? It is easy to imagine advances in virtual and extended reality revolutionizing many of the interactions people have in shopping, learning, and working environments—as well as, of course, entertainment. Up to now, extended reality has primarily been used in gaming applications to create more immersive experiences for players. As the technology evolved and gained popularity, research and development started happening within and on behalf of other consumer-facing businesses, such as retailers, and these organizations are experimenting with extended reality in many ways. Marketers of goods from high-end wristwatches and trendy eyeglasses to furniture and building supplies—and even cosmetics—have already given customers the ability to "try before they buy" via their smartphones.[4]

To be sure, technological advances will keep coming, and great business strategists will continue to capitalize on them. Alignment of intelligent automation with the business strategy starts with the right questions: Where does top management want to take the organization in this era of intelligent automation? What is the future of the industry? Will that change how value is defined three to five years from now? Only with a clear sense of strategy can a management team think holistically about all the systems, resources, constraints, boundaries, and components that must be aligned.

Strategy for Automation at Scale

It is crucial for an organization's business imperatives to be translated into an automation strategy. Automation, after all, is a large realm of activity, with a finite set of resources being devoted to it and a need to produce maximum value. So far, we've been discussing business strategies supported *with* intelligent automation. It is also essential for executives and managers to be able to express their intelligent automation strategy *for systems*. To be sure, systems strategy must always be vertically aligned to business strategy; it should never work at cross-purposes to what the business is trying to achieve. Still, it deserves to be mapped out in its own right, with the intent of building powerful and sustained capabilities across the enterprise.

Specifically, with regard to automation, we know that certain foundational elements must be put in place before benefits can be derived from robotic process automation, intelligent automation, or AI. A well-thought-out intelligent automation strategy begins with an honest assessment of where a company is in its journey—including the state of its data. (As Watts Humphrey, the "father of software quality" and pioneer of the maturity model, put it: "If you don't know where you are, a map won't help."[5]) Then from that point, it lays out a pathway to building additional capabilities and reaping higher levels of value from investments in automation technology. It should map out timelines and provide guidance on how accountability will be ensured and returns on investment tracked.

Like business strategies, systems strategies can vary dramatically from organization to organization. And even when companies invest heavily in a variety of technologies, the outcomes can be disappointing. Investments in key technology, while necessary, aren't enough to ensure market leadership. Fragmented investments result in too many disparate systems operating in technology silos. These silos often preclude collaboration between various parts of the business, and fragmented decision-making seldom reflects strategic business goals. To be a market leader, a company should, from the start, have in mind a larger strategy for future-ready systems.

Technical information is doubling every two years. The implication is that half of what is relevant at any given point in time may be outdated two years later. But conventional systems—that is, software applications, hardware, data centers, and so forth—were not built for the current world of the Internet of Things, sensors, mobile computing, AI applications, and billions of devices. Nor were they designed to evolve for the world of tomorrow, whatever that might be. Traditionally, the components of the IT "stack"—database, applications, and infrastructure—have been treated as independent entities. The divisions are fading, with organizations moving to the cloud, uniform approach for data, security, and governance.

As the technology landscape of every organization grows, systems should be designed to be interoperable to realize the full potential of the technology. Unnecessary dependencies across all layers of the solution stack should be removed to avoid inefficiencies and redundancies. The overall business model should be redesigned, with new partnerships as necessary, to cultivate a future-proof ecosystem.

The future of technology will only bring more change—and not at a constant rate. Systems should be architected to seamlessly handle disruptions and insulated against change using flexible architectures. The approach should be to identify the biggest friction points in a business that are slowing down adoption and value realization. A company must work on its data strategy, starting with quality data and applying a data-centric approach to its most important business decisions. It must put humans at the center of its process designs, recognizing that data and technology will not alone solve problems.

As discussed in Chapter 2, organizational and cultural barriers will have to be broken down, starting with a close scrutiny of how they are hindering speed and accountability. The thinking behind the phrase "fail fast, experiment early" is that teams should expose their designs to feedback in early stages, learn from the failures, and produce a series of iterations that show continuous and stable improvement—this is the best way not only to achieve the full possibilities of an emerging technology but also to socialize the change involved. It's a good way, too, to learn sooner rather than later if corporate policies around data or other matters will present hurdles to the solution an automation team is trying to build.

A well-devised intelligent automation strategy will help a company's executives and managers drive this change. Asking three questions at regular intervals can help keep an automation strategy on track: Are we focusing on establishing an *automation ecosystem* that breaks down the organizational silos and optimizes our investment? Is our strategy focusing on being *truly agile* and allowing fast decision-making to respond quickly to the technology changes? And are we designing automation to *scale across the enterprise*, with systems that pave the way to the future?

Any organization formulating a future-proof automation strategy should aim to:

- ▶ Cultivate a well-structured automation ecosystem in which networks of partners, service providers, and academic institutions together create value.
- ▶ Build to a scale that will allow the company to innovate rapidly and with confidence—and roll out solutions with real impact.
- ▶ Leverage prebuilt, customizable solutions, designed to plug into and across the enterprise, accelerate innovation across functions, drive down costs, and get to outcomes faster.
- ▶ Underpin automation strategy with a robust data strategy. For example, having autonomous data integration— including real-time data at the edge—can create a single "source of truth" to guide a business.

For many businesses, devising a sound automation strategy will involve serious thought about the right strategic partnerships to forge to support the launch and scaling of new capabilities and ventures. Often, an exciting opportunity exists that cannot be made into reality unless the offering can be operated at substantial scale. But considering the pace at which the technology is changing, there might not be enough time for a company to scale up an offering, especially if that requires developing certain capabilities in-house. Even if the development of such capabilities is done in time, building market recognition for those capabilities will be a challenge.

The fastest way to scale is therefore building strong strategic partnerships with niche players that already have the market recognition for building such products and capabilities. Take the extended reality opportunities just discussed. Most companies investing in these possibilities for enhanced customer experience are partnering with firms that are long experienced and positioned as leaders in the virtual reality space, and see themselves as players in an extensive ecosystem that they will continue to tap to produce next-level immersive experiences.

Depending on the financials and long-term trajectory, some companies determine that it is the right strategic move to acquire these small, niche kinds of players because their technology can be instrumental to strengthening the strategic position of the business. Others work on bringing various stakeholders, partners, and customers onto a single platform so that they can benefit from a seamless flow of data and feedback, fueling the growth of the business.

Simple, Seamless, Scaled, Sustained

Turning an intelligent automation strategy into reality requires a structured approach to ensure that business leaders, IT leaders, and employees throughout the ranks travel together in that journey. An easy-to-remember model based on four Ss—it is simple, seamless, scaled, and sustained—can help guide decisions along the way (see Figure 3.1).

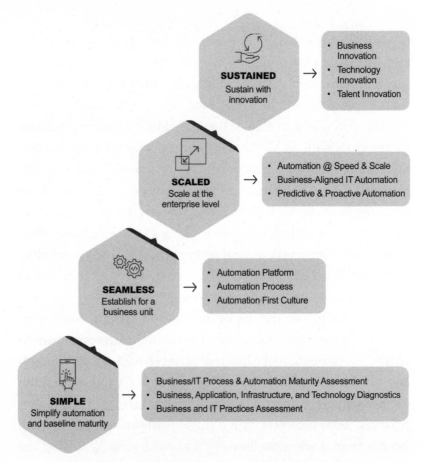

FIGURE 3.1 "Four S" Strategy Drives to Achieve the Highest Automation Maturity Level

Simple

One of the most famous quotes from Henry David Thoreau's *Walden* is this: "Our life is frittered away by detail. . . . Simplicity, simplicity, simplicity! I say." The same goes for automation solutions. Simple is a principle that says we should look for ways to reduce the crazy-quilt complexity of existing processes or systems. Instead of adding to that complexity barrier with every new project, we should retool applications and architectures for simple modularity.

The principle of simplification should be applied at three levels: first, by identifying the use cases that matter to the business—that is, identifying ROI-driven automation use cases; second, by designing automation that is easy to use, easy to scale, and easy to evolve; and third, by taking a practical implementation approach, where every user is assisted in seamlessly integrating automation into their day-to-day life

Simplification also means streamlining a business process prior to automating it in part or whole. Do this by applying Lean principles and Six Sigma to eliminate unnecessary or overly convoluted work steps. Recall the cardinal rule from Chapter 2: do not automate a poorly designed process—or the wrong steps will just be done faster. The right approach is to optimize the process and then pause before jumping into an automation solution that others have used. What was right for one organization may be more complex than another organization is ready to address. Figuring out where a given organization is on its automation journey is a very important step.

More simple advice: automation leaders should perform a baselining and benchmarking exercise so they know where their organizations are in the process and how they are progressing. Along with this, they should establish approaches for reporting, governance, and tracking benefits. It's all very basic, yet very critical.

Seamless

The second important principle revolves around ensuring seamlessness between the existing technology ecosystem and the automation layer. If a company is using ServiceNow, for example, its automation enablement must be in line with its ServiceNow strategy. If it is using an ELK stack (comprises three popular open-source projects: Elasticsearch, Logstash, and Kibana) as an open-source software for analytics and AI, it needs to have open-source plug-and-play APIs to which it can connect. It needs to integrate its automation layer using APIs, microservices, and containers, as opposed to pushing one more tool or asset into the existing technology environment. A seamless, accurate data fabric is also critical.

Success in the future will depend on seamlessly connecting core systems with the new through digital decoupling. Think about the strategy of some of today's fastest-growing companies, such as Amazon, to function as platforms—making the structures and capabilities they built to support their own operations available to other businesses looking for efficient ways to serve customers.

Within a company, automation can adopt that same model, creating a platform that individual solutions can utilize and that allows them to work together. When we talk about *seamless,* we are also talking about providing a seamless automated experience for end users—something that becomes a bit easier when a company takes a greenfield approach to enterprise architecture. Most enterprises today, however, rely on incumbent systems of technologies that were originally designed just for utility. These are simply inadequate to support the rate of innovation most companies must achieve to address changing customer expectations. Any system created from a clean slate today would be designed first and foremost to deliver a smooth end-user experience, while allowing for constant integrations of new technologies and changes to business processes—and while not jeopardizing the essential utility required.

Making automation seamless within an IT organization also has a cultural element. Part of the change management side of intelligent automation is getting leadership and employees to embrace the idea that the work of automation is never finished. People should always be asking: What can we automate next?

It has been said that the world's most inventive and future-ready companies have a certain DNA—deep differences in how they think and work that are hard for others to copy.[6] Shifting an organization to an automation-first culture requires sustained emphasis on encouraging, celebrating, and equipping people for ongoing learning, incremental prototyping, cocreation (e.g., through hackathons and design thinking workshops), and other aspects of continuous improvement and innovation. It doesn't happen overnight, but instilling the DNA of innovation in an organization will allow it to accomplish all the building, scaling, and innovating required across an extended automation journey.

Scaled

Once a team has designed an automation solution and seen proof of concept in a small-scale, experimental setting, the challenge is to roll it out to work at industrial scale and in real-world conditions, day after day, with reliability. Scaling an intelligent automation solution requires five sets of issues to be addressed: business readiness; data access and governance; culture and talent; platforms and architecture; and issues specific to intelligent automation (such as tracking emerging technologies and having a platform mindset).

An important point here is that scaling should not be a "big bang" switchover. It should be done with a wave approach, steadily building capability and expertise. Scaling AI and automation capabilities at an enterprise level requires a holistic strategy that cuts across all types of talent segments and skills.

As Chapter 7 discusses in detail, talent development is a big part of scaling. Automation cannot be just a small team's responsibility. It has to be everyone's responsibility within the enterprise. Investing in skills at an enterprise level, therefore, is crucial to get the organization ready for the future and to build these capabilities at scale.

Sustained

Finally, it is essential that companies do not see automation as a one-and-done initiative. To preserve the edge in a rapidly changing business environment, they must keep pushing it forward. One implication of this is that a company should put mechanisms in place to continuously scan industry research, identify emerging possibilities with robotic process automation, other types of automation, AI, and analytics—and investigate how other organizations are experimenting with them.

To remain relevant, companies must stay on top of market trends, customer behavior patterns, and emerging ways of working. Change comes fast, not only to products and offerings, but also to operating models and automation strategies. Managers have to revisit on a regular basis the decisions they have made, and consider whether and how to invest their limited resources in promising automation areas and AI technologies. Staying relevant is a function of predicting what can be predicted about the future, redirecting investments, and pivoting to new opportunities and growth areas.

More important still, an organization should have ways of inspiring and harvesting automation ideas from everyone in its ranks. No one knows better than the worker involved day-to-day in a process where the friction points are and how their time could be better spent. Whether through hackathons, jams, AI-athons, or any other participative initiative, people should be given ways to speak up and to be heard when they see opportunities. Management needs to achieve a degree of "industrialization" of automation that everyone in the organization supports. The goal is for everyone to agree it is vital to look for new opportunities for automation to reduce costs, increase speed to market, or achieve some other business priority more effectively.

Finally, sustaining efforts in intelligent automation depends on having a way to monitor the business value being produced. Even when automation solutions are well aligned with business goals and priorities, if their actual value creation is not tracked, then further funding may be cut off. Being careful to account for every dollar of investment and savings can do a lot to sustain support for intelligent automation and recognition of the value generated by it.

How It Looks in Practice

The story of one financial services company we know well should help bring some of the concepts we've been discussing to life.

Recognizing that customer behavior was evolving in terms of people's preferences for interacting with service firms, this company decided to launch a new wealth management advisory service supported by intelligent automation. The goal was twofold: first, to grow its customer base by growing a new market of people who in the past had not had access to affordable, highly tailored financial advice, and second, to retain sophisticated customers at risk of migrating to other providers if those other companies were able to offer convenient automated solutions first.

To stay ahead of the curve, business leaders at the bank began by familiarizing themselves with the state of the art in other industries' applications of automation, and imagining how similar tools might allow it to reinvent its offerings and interactions with customers. Then with those creative opportunities in mind, the bank devised an automation strategy to design and develop the innovations and launch them into the mass retail banking market.

Guided at every level by the North Star of strategic intent, the automation initiative had a holistic perspective from the outset. It envisioned the implications for other lines of business, interdependent processes, data management, and talent management. Questions relating to how the content of certain jobs might change, and how to reskill and upskill current staff, weren't afterthoughts—they were raised early and addressed thoughtfully.

It was around this point that we became acquainted with the effort, as Accenture was engaged to help design, build, and test the new advisory solution, using an Agile methodology featuring rapid development of a minimum viable product and subsequent iterations to refine it based on feedback. The product was then tested in the market, where customers were able to access the online service 24/7 and were asked to complete a thorough questionnaire about the experience of using it. The new, automated wealth advisor showed great promise for public adoption. And indeed, today this solution is operating at scale, offering wealth management advice to the bank's customers and making new inroads into underserved markets.

What makes this digital financial advisor succeed? Fundamentally, the AI embedded in it delivers sound advice. In the blink of an eye, its algorithms serve up answers on a par with those a veteran advisor in the bank would offer. Just as important, the tool is simple and intuitive to use, thanks to detailed assessments of customer experience and usage requirements. After taking a customer through a series of questions about finances, investment experience, and risk appetite, it recommends a personalized investment portfolio of stocks, bonds, and other asset types. The story ends in a classic win-win outcome: customers gain round-the-clock access to reliable financial guidance, and the bank emerges as a digital innovation leader.

The Role of Leadership

Strategy and leadership are often mentioned in the same breath, and there is a reason for that. Senior leaders own the strategy-making process. Solutions take shape fastest when leaders in an organization decide to prioritize them. No strategy succeeds without people articulating it clearly to their colleagues, making daily decisions in line with it, and generally driving what is often a complex change process.

The fact is that intelligent automation should be approached as an enterprisewide initiative, in much the same way that companies have learned to envision the digital transformation of the whole business rather than invest in projects to digitize this and that in various corners. If the hope is—as it should be—to gain a competitive edge through investments in automation, they should be approached strategically, implemented holistically, and managed consistently. Second, this implies a level of priority setting for intelligent automation projects that can only emanate from top management. And if funding decisions need to be made at the level of the C-suite, top leadership must be on board, understanding and helping others understand how intelligent automation allows the business to meet its goals and thrive in ever-changing and always challenging markets.

Because intelligent automation should be an enterprisewide strategy, having top executives make the case for automation is especially important. Instead of applying automation in pieces—a predictive model here, a virtual agent or chatbot there—leaders should strategize at the enterprise level about how automation will be introduced and scaled across lines of business, projects, run support, infrastructure, digital, security, and so on. It is the leader's job to set the strategy, communicate it through the organization, and keep progress toward it on track.

This chapter has emphasized some key points about strategy and strategic intent around intelligent automation. Most important to appreciate is that everything proceeds from the strategic intent of the business. For intelligent automation to drive a competitive advantage or have transformative impact, it must directly support an important point of differentiation. When automation is guided by strategic purpose, it can do wonders for a company's performance; if it isn't, it can amount to little more than added overhead cost.

The question a company should begin with is: What intelligent automation initiatives will do most to help us achieve the competitive positioning we want in the market? But strategic thinking is needed at other levels, too. Intelligent automation becomes a source of ongoing advantage when managers have a long-term map of the automation journey ahead, and invest in a portfolio of projects that build a well-integrated environment with systems that will enable success in the future. Individual solutions achieve their highest returns when they are thoughtfully planned, resourced, and guided by unambiguous goals.

Key Takeaways

▸ Any intelligent automation effort should align with the strategy of the business. Focus on solving problems that have real impact on enterprise success.

▸ Projects should also fit into a mapped-out strategy for building up the intelligent automation capability of the organization. Early efforts should lay the groundwork for later ones.

▸ At the individual project level too, an automation initiative needs a strategy. Set motivating goals and translate those into clear timelines.

▸ Because strategy evolves constantly in response to changing conditions, there must be a process for periodically revisiting and refreshing an organization's intelligent automation strategy.

4

Choose Your Spots and Map Your Journey

A few years ago, the chief information officer (CIO) of a large enterprise we know was seeking to improve automation's impact on their business.

Across a series of acquisitions, both big and small, headquarters functions had, for various reasons, avoided the complicated challenge of integrating business units and as a result, operated as a decentralized group of units. With little to no communications among business units, there were wheels being reinvented by business and IT staff in different places.

Like many IT executives, the CIO was looking for more clarity and visibility into what was happening on the ground but knew there must be countless opportunities for automating mind-numbing, error-prone processes. In this new digital era, the CIO wanted to move the IT operations unit away from being a traditional cost center to become a business value driver. To that effect, the CIO initiated a chain of conversations with other members of the C-suite to bridge the gap between IT strategy and the overall business strategy of the organization.

Seeking to improve application stability and operational efficiency, the company undertook an automation assessment to help identify the greatest opportunities to achieve its business goals. Certain efforts were prioritized based on their synergistic potential, and the results of the assessment pointed to the potential to achieve a 45 percent reduction in incident volume and up to a 60 percent effort reduction in their regular operations. The company also was in line to save substantial costs for software tool licenses, achieve 99 percent business operations stability, and reach 98 percent compliance with service-level agreements with its customers.

These were all cost-saving initiatives, however—a focus that might be fine for the traditional cost center, but recall that this CIO wanted to generate value for the business. So he undertook an exhaustive assessment of the company's business processes. He included business stakeholders, industry experts, and technology architects in an enterprisewide attempt to eliminate redundant work, streamline critical activities, and boost the potential for business value creation in every process.

Once a leaner set of business processes had been established, he worked with automation architects and integration engineers to automate 40 percent of the business operations, thereby deriving tremendous value for the organization. Since then, to keep pace with the ever-changing technology landscape, the CIO has constantly reevaluated automation prospects at regular intervals. This is an environment of continuous improvement, in which people have grown accustomed to facing the technology tide in a proactive manner.

At the outset, it was very hard to know where and how to start. Indeed, this is a major challenge for many companies:

determining just what to automate first, next, and then after that. In a world of scarce budgetary resources, IT organizational capacity, and managerial attention, there must be a rational way to make these decisions.

The CIO's company is a good example of an organization that had many competing opportunities and proliferating intelligent automation solutions, but lacked central coordination or confidence that it was investing in line with strategic priorities. With a centrally coordinated leadership, however, intelligent automation can do wonders for traditional businesses.

Today, most companies are deploying technologies in pockets of their organizations, without a vision for scaling the innovation from these technologies across the enterprise. They may be chasing exciting possibilities, proving concepts, engaging people in pilots at many levels—but they are not managing or monitoring the collective impact of these initiatives, or even supporting shared learning across projects.

Too often, teams run into difficulties with scaling because they have not vetted opportunities wisely in the first place and focused their efforts on the best ones. Without overarching business priorities guiding these projects, they do not add up to more than the sum of their parts. In some cases, they may not even pay their own way, because they expend efforts on automating processes that were not well designed in the first place.

If a management team is serious about realizing the potential of intelligent automation, it needs a way of identifying opportunities that are data driven—quantitative as well as qualitative. This will help it zero in on those opportunities that are both high value in terms of their probable business impact and well matched to the organization's current level of automation maturity.

Leaders need to ask: What, from a business-centric perspective, would be most impactful to automate? Then: What form of automation would be feasible, given our capacity to develop and deploy solutions? And given the answers to those questions: As we map out a plan for automation that represents a valuable automation journey—with increasing capabilities and momentum toward greater automation successes in the future—what makes sense to put in place first? And what next?

This chapter takes those questions in turn, sharing the approach that has worked in many company settings. First, it involves identifying processes that are valuable candidates for automation, both because they are vital to the organization's performance and because they involve repetitive, routine information-handling tasks. Second, it calls for a clear-eyed assessment of a company's automation maturity and therefore readiness to take on automation initiatives of different levels of sophistication. Finally, it leads to constructing a road map for undertaking initiatives in a productive sequence, so that each builds on what has been done previously. This helps the organization to steadily grow its intelligent automation capabilities and achieve maximum benefit for the business.

Identifying Opportunities: What Offers the Greatest Impact?

Chapter 3 discussed the need to align strategy with business priorities—and to understand at the outset how automation should make the enterprise more successful.

Will it be by boosting the top line by creating new offerings and customer-facing capabilities that generate revenues? Or will it be by improving efficiency of existing processes and applying automation to reduce the expensive involvement of people? Is intelligent automation the answer to greater speed, lower cost, or better service? Having clarity on this up front allows potential use cases to be mapped against the current corporate strategy and specific opportunities to be prioritized—whether the goal is to catch up with rivals or gain new advantages over them.

At one luxury automaker, for example, the major business goal behind an intelligent automation effort was to achieve higher productivity in manufacturing through the proactive prevention of stoppages. Every project entails a cost, so the imperative is to look at projected ROI. There must be a business case for any automation with financial return considerations and also broader business value considerations.

Translating strategic business goals to automation initiatives means focusing on business processes. Usually it is not hard to find labor-intensive work processes that seem to cry out for automated solutions. In business-process-intense industries like mortgage processing, some are not worth automating, or at least not automating as-is; they often need to be optimized. Some work needs to simply be eradicated. As work turns to identifying work processes that should be targeted for automation, we often use a framework: eradicate and optimize—and only then, automate. It's a simple mantra, but at the same time important enough to spend some paragraphs unpacking.

Eradicate the Unnecessary

Let's begin with the work that should simply be swept aside. Just because managers discover a corner of operations where people are being asked to do mind-numbing work doesn't mean that an automation solution is called for. It could be that the work should not be done at all.

Any readers of this book already trained in management techniques like Lean process improvement or Six Sigma defect reduction will recognize that this is a common refrain in those methodologies.[1] The typical company does a lot of unnecessary work, and some of it could be avoided if someone paused to ask, "Why are we doing this?"

Consider the example of a large bank's IT operations. Like all banks, this one has systems containing batch applications for updating information at the end of the day, generating reports, printing documents, and other noninteractive tasks that must be completed reliably within certain business deadlines. It had over 75,000 batch jobs executed on a monthly basis. But it was experiencing a very high level of failures, which required manual interventions from skilled IT professionals.

Given the types of failures—there were multiple repetitive failures occurring under certain business and data conditions—it seemed valuable to look into automating the kinds of fixes these professionals were making. Indeed, the bank went some distance down that path by pursuing forms of shift-left enablement—that is, making it possible for lower-level service agents (rather than the more expert ones to the right of them on the organizational chart) to handle a problem. Shift-left adjustments often involve updating standard operating procedures (SOPs) and providing these to the level one (L1) IT services team.

But this was not a sufficient or the best solution. The much better question to ask was: What is *causing* these failures? It turned out the code was flawed in various ways. In many cases, a simple code fix could eliminate the failures upstream. Within four months, the project team was able to apply 250 permanent fixes. This reduced the incidents in production by 46 percent and along with that, the draw on skilled IT workers' time. No need to automate those fixes if the problems aren't occurring.

That example teaches the value of eradicating work wherever it is unnecessary rather than automating. It also shows how to do it, by drilling down into the underlying causes of high-volume problems that seem like candidates for automation. Using what is known as *root cause analysis* is the best way to find inefficiencies.[2]

Within the IT realm, much of the source of unnecessary processes and work is the technical debt that has built up in legacy production environments. Software developers working under tight deadlines make enhancements in the form of patches to a system and rarely get around to revisiting underlying code. Systems therefore grow into increasingly Byzantine-like structures, pocked with redundancies, dead code, and obsolete code. The debt accumulating over time, as minimal application rationalization and performance tuning effort is applied, comes in the form of rising maintenance work and cost—and like the national debt of many countries, it only seems to go up with the passing years, never down. A lot of times, the best path to greater efficiency is not the seemingly direct one of automating a high volume of work tasks, but the effort to prune these tangled roots.

Examples of successful intelligent automation abound in the IT realm, but hardly end there. Think of a recent transformation in the world of print media. Traditionally, many publishers have always depended on advertising revenues. From the earliest days of newspapers, they have placed printed advertisements alongside articles, creating a distracting nuisance for news consumers and detracting from the overall reading experience. This has carried over to the digital world, and even as advertisers shift their budgets to search engines, content publishers continue to load up on embedded advertisements.

New automation technologies, however, are changing this game for printed newspapers, by enabling highly targeted insertions of supplemental sections. What these advertising sections lose in proximity to the content most capturing readers' attention, they make up in more highly relevant ads, matched to the consumer's specific geography and demographics. This allows, for example, a local restaurant to advertise in a national newspaper, sending out holiday offers to households in their vicinity. And because these arrive as insertions in newspapers, they avoid the cost of delivering flyers by mail. This innovation is opening additional sources of revenue for print media companies and helping counter the threat of digital publishers' ability to serve customized ads on screens.

At the same time, print publishers are using automation to streamline the process of verifying and reporting circulation numbers—essential information for sales and sales forecasting. Process automation yields data capture that eradicates layers of manual data collection and analysis. And the vast resource of historical data about content published, circulation revenues, and advertising revenues supports projections that can factor in foreseeable local events like a local team competing in a championship or an upcoming regional festival.

Our favorite example is from a client we serve, which had a monthly process that used to take 17 days to finish. It was one of many processes under consideration for automation, and given its interdependencies with many other applications, it would have taken considerable effort to transform and optimize. But going through the list of candidates, the client hinted that this was a very old application and might not have many users. We turned on the user logging and found that was correct: in fact, *zero* users had accessed the application data in the past six months. Within one week, the decision was made to decommission the application. (As reengineering guru Michael Hammer once put it: Don't automate—obliterate!) More important, the incident got the company more focused on technical debt, and between efforts on that side and 150 tweaks to optimize performance of other applications, its batch execution window time overall was slashed by 30 percent—before automating anything.

Optimize the Process

Say a set of work steps can't be eradicated; the process is necessary to perform. Very likely, it is just not an immediate candidate for automation even though, as it exists today, it is performing suboptimally. There may be redundant steps in it or weak points that make it failure prone.

To optimize a process, the first step is to map it. If a team has never done this, it might want to start with small and simple processes—and even then, it may be surprised. A process that looks straightforward can actually be rife with exceptions and special cases, all of which have to be anticipated and documented. Even if members of the team have mapped processes before, the fact that this time the goal is to identify automation opportunities will bring extra complexity.

One essential piece of advice is to map a process not simply based on a worker's logical description of it, but by observing the process in action. Surprisingly, there often is a real difference between the official process people will claim to adhere to and the unofficial one they actually use. Then, after the steps have been sketched as observed, it's important to double-check the process by walking people through it and by going back to see again if people actually follow those steps in that order. The process map document should be revised till it truly reflects the reality. Any process automation choices made should be based on how people are in fact doing their work and not the idealized process that some manager in the past thought they should follow.

Once the process is mapped out accurately, and assuming it's been discovered that all or part of it could be handled by smart machines, it's time to face the question: Is this process *worth* automating? And is it worth automating as-is—or does the process itself need to be redesigned before being automated? Recall the point made in Chapter 2: a poorly designed process is a barrier to automation. Once handed over to machines, it will just race through the wrong steps more quickly. Automation can't be a Band-Aid for a bad process. It shouldn't be applied to a mediocre workflow and expected to yield a triumph of efficiency.

If the process is worth automating, but not as-is, a proven methodology such as Lean process improvement can be used to make it better. Taking what it has seen and heard, the team should consider if it can make the process better by identifying bottlenecks and other problematic steps in the process—which if addressed will go a long way to streamlining the process. Streamlining also comes from identifying parts of the process that can be accelerated or performed congruently instead of linearly. Part of applying Lean principles to a process will be a focus on combining or cutting process steps that are only slowing things down.

All this should be done with the involvement of subject matter experts—that is, the nontechnical, business-side, constant users of the process. The team already worked with them iteratively to map the existing process; now it can come back to them to introduce the revised process map, get their feedback, and iterate again to make it even better. For the subject matter experts, the final version of the process document should be the basis of a new standard operating procedure (SOP) document, used to train new hires in the future. Note that automation has not come into the picture yet. The first priority is making sure the process efficiently accomplishes its purpose. Having streamlined it by eliminating unnecessary steps, only then should the focus turn to automating the process in part or in whole.

But keep in mind the possibility that the process still should not be automated at all. There are various reasons that a process might not be a good choice for automation despite appearing so at first glance. It might have so many small process steps or involve so much complexity that it would take a lot of time to automate, for small payback. It might also be that, in the course of studying the process, it becomes clear that the automated part would only be needed to occur a few times a month—again, making it not much of a savings of workers' time. This is part of why the initial hunt for automation applications should be expansive; they won't all pan out. Even so, the effort is valuable. Any work on process mapping and refinement makes the work more efficient and less onerous for the people doing it.

Automate the Work

Only after a team has improved the process should it proceed to automate it. We'll discuss the very important task of prioritizing among the processes that have been identified. For now, the assumption is that work is going forward with a chosen project. At this point, two basic questions arise: Will the automation be full or partial? And how simple or complex should the automation solution be?

Processes, of course, consist of individual tasks, which are more or less amenable to automation. It is very common that only parts of the process will be automated. Although sophisticated intelligent automation can optimize highly complex processes, make decisions, self-correct, and even understand context, some tasks remain dependent upon human judgment and are therefore incompatible with even the most leading-edge automation.

Consider BNY Mellon, which has deployed hundreds of bots across its business to drive efficiency and cut out costly errors. One cadre of robotic assistants, for example, is accelerating the bank's critical payment processing by reducing the time spent by employees identifying and dealing with data mistakes. Yet the employees are still in place, handling the exceptions where judgment has to be brought to bear.[3]

Finding the activities in the process that can be well handled by intelligent automation and AI depends on having awareness of evolving solution possibilities. What quickly becomes clear is that there are a range of technical offerings on the market, and they range from the very simple to the very complex.

In our own work, we find it useful to classify solutions into three basic groups according to whether their application will be simple, involve medium complexity, or involve high complexity. A simple solution usually requires process change, but beyond that has an off-the-shelf quality that makes implementation relatively straightforward. A medium-complexity solution requires building a custom solution, whether using robotic process automation or another automation approach. A high-complexity solution requires integration of two or more preexisting systems, themselves already complex.

Which way should a given team go? Clearly, if the choice is there, it should opt for the simplest solution that is less disruptive and designed to take advantage of existing tools and technology. But this doesn't mean shying away from projects with complexity levels that will challenge an organization in a productive way and build its capacities to automate for higher impact.

Choose Wisely

In general, the applications that present themselves as automation opportunities will have some common characteristics: they may require frequent and manual updates, rapid scaling, data extracts, or a high degree of personalization.

If an application relies on data, it is a natural candidate for AI, such as machine learning for self-evolution. Management should resist the temptation, however, to greenlight too many projects. It shouldn't become so enamored of emerging technologies that it invests in automation for automation's sake. Keep in mind that just because a process is important and can be automated doesn't mean it has to be automated at a high level.

We heard, for example, about a restaurant chain that was exploring AI-enabled chatbots to collect customer feedback. A sophisticated chatbot could do that, certainly. But many restaurants have an app on a mobile device that's handed to customers after their meal to provide feedback. If that software is accomplishing the task perfectly well, is there really a need for AI?

The key here is to look for friction points where the improvement in performance on recurring tasks will have the most impact on business success, and therefore where use of automation assets and tools will be most valuable. For example, within IT services, one automaker was getting customer complaints. It found a key cause was the time it took to respond to customer issues—and spotted a good opportunity for automation. After it implemented an automated application management solution, it reduced the resolution time to respond to customer issues by 50 percent and saw a 20 percent reduction in complaints. This improved customer satisfaction and significantly reduced the escalation that had been occurring, all the way to the CIO's level.

Sometimes these friction points can be discovered with data analytics. Deep dive analytics using trends, text analytics, web analytics, social media analytics, predictions, and what-if scenarios can provide insights to drive more automation and optimization opportunities. This brings a scientific, data-driven approach that improves on the traditional methods of interviews and questionnaires to understand opportunities, not to mention that it sets up a way to track the actual impact to the business after a solution is implemented.

The top candidates should be chosen based on potential impact. Again, a good process improvement methodology such as Lean management or Six Sigma helps point the way. An analysis using Six Sigma's "cause and effect matrix" can reveal processes that should take priority based on criteria, including their frequency, effort required to automate, criticality to the business, and potential time savings. Once values are assigned to each of these factors, it is a simple matter of using the matrix to calculate totals and determine how high on the list of potential automation projects a given process should go.

Another useful tool for prioritizing among candidate projects is the kind of matrix shown in Figure 4.1. It calls for plotting every project's position on the grid by considering, first, how hard it would be to build (the y-axis) and second, how important its impact would be to the business. Projects that are relatively easy to build and have relatively high impact, for example, land in the lower right quadrant labeled "quick wins." Projects that fall into the same range of relative high impacts but are harder to build are those in the top right quadrant, and more likely to represent strategic bets—not only because their complexity brings higher risk but also because a success in this realm would be more likely to confer a more enduring competitive edge.

In the example shown in the figure, an IT services group has sorted its identified opportunities across the matrix. It will now proceed to create a road map that envisions the accomplishment of many of the high-complexity/high-impact projects. Organizations can prioritize solutions by weighing factors such as complexity to build versus positive impacts and the ability to control/manage versus negative impacts.

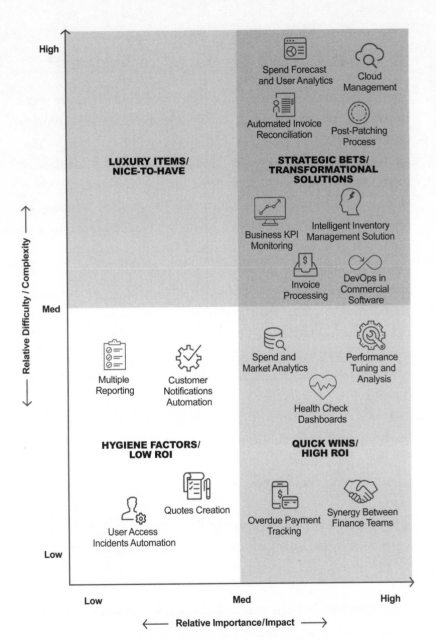

FIGURE 4.1 Matrix for Prioritizing Options

Assessing Maturity: What Are We Prepared to Address?

The second major factor to take into account in choosing spots for intelligent automation is an organization's level of automation maturity.

Maturity is vital to understand because people's capabilities to tackle a project very much affect its risk-and-reward profile. In other words, perhaps an idea has huge potential, but can the organization pull it off? Does it actually have the experience and skills—as well as the resources and foundations in place—to put it in place as an automation solution? What foundational capabilities already exist? Before making choices among competing project ideas, managers should take time to determine the organization's current maturity in terms of the automation maturity index.

Remember the stages noted in Chapter 1. Companies go through five basic phases:

1. Foundation (tools driven): Automation at this level is more individually focused, siloed, and with a fragmented set of tools that provide point solutions.

2. Optimize (process driven): Elimination of unnecessary process steps, and optimization and improvement of the processes.

3. Efficient (robotic process automation driven): Focus on automating all repetitive tasks that can be quick wins in automation, and establish and stabilize all the foundational activities that are prerequisites for data-driven and intelligent automation.

4. Predictive (data driven): Shift the focus from cost reduction to improved efficiency and differentiated experience. The next major step is to derive the insights and intelligence from data to drive automation for business to be agile and predictable.

5. Intelligent (AI driven): Allows machines to sense, comprehend, act, and learn. AI can take automation beyond merely rules-based work, right into the areas we currently believe always need human judgment.

Automation maturity assessment is basically an exercise in benchmarking, comparing what one's own company is doing and capable of doing with what can be observed at peer companies. It entails identifying the AI and analytics capabilities the company uses today, and then doing a capabilities and gap analysis. Most companies, frankly, overestimate their maturity, because they have not worked to fully understand the advantages that AI can provide, such as making decisions, discovering opportunities for innovation, and creating capabilities for self-evolution. Good questions to ask are: How would we build our company differently to take advantage of these? And how different is that vision from how the company is built today?

Since the retail industry is familiar to most people, let's use it to imagine how organizations of different maturity levels might be automating parts of their business. A retailer with foundational automation would be one that is running a basic ecommerce site. This means it has basic competence with interface design and order process automation—and plenty of transaction data to manage. One maturity level up, another retailer might be applying robotic process automation to various parts of its operation, such as in checking inventory levels and preparing routine orders to be placed with vendors. An even more mature retail organization would meanwhile be using analytics, perhaps to support better decision-making by its merchandisers by predicting demand for new product launches.

Now step up to the maturity level of a retailer that is applying intelligent automation. This retailer might add a chatbot to its online customer interface, capable of offering solutions to a customer's problem with an awareness of that customer's loyalty and lifetime value to the company. Finally, at the highest automation maturity level, a leading-edge retailer would have infused its intelligent automation with AI capabilities. As just one possibility, it might integrate machine learning into its cybersecurity defenses, allowing for automatic detection and response to novel methods being used by hackers.

It is important to stress, however, that despite the emphasis in this example on technology solutions, an organization's automation maturity depends on more than its technology capabilities and track record. To get a full view of maturity, managers need to consider other factors as well. They'll need a combination of data assessment, technology assessment, process assessment, and culture assessment. Together, these determine automation maturity and expose the gaps to meet the business objectives and priorities (see Figure 4.2.)

If you think about combining multiple assessments along these lines, it is possible to imagine creating an automation maturity index that combines them all with appropriate weighting and can be used to score not only an entire organization, but any process or subprocess within it. For different industry verticals or technology groups, the weightages of these multiple people, process, and technology parameters would undoubtedly vary. This would suggest that benchmarking within an organization's industry would be valuable, as it would indicate that organization's distance from the most relevant automation leaders and the areas to focus on to match their current maturity.

BUSINESS-IT
PRIORITY
ALIGNMENT
Assess business
to IT alignment

APPLICATION
AND ARCHITECTURE
ASSESSMENT
Assess application
landscape categorization and
architecture flexibility

CULTURE
Assess current
maturity of the project
on automation and tools

AUTOMATION
ASSESSMENT

DATA
Use historical data
for insights into
delivery and business
focus areas

TOOL LANDSCAPE
Create a tools blueprint to
complete the ecosystem
based on assessments

PROCESS
Conduct a deep study of the
project's processes, such as
incident, problem, change,
service requests,
and SLAs

FIGURE 4.2   **Components Evaluated in an Automation Opportunity Identification Assessment**

The assessment covers the people, process, and technology aspects of the organization to discover and design a sustainable and evolving automation ecosystem. It helps answer a big question: Where are we in the automation journey? It is very important that the organization start with understanding where it is in the automation journey by benchmarking and baselining, using a reference framework like a maturity framework or a quantitative index. Once it knows where it is, it can easily draw and follow a road map to where it wants to be.

This is an ongoing effort, especially as each solution implemented builds maturity and makes further solutions possible. For example, one financial services company used intelligent automation to boost the effectiveness of its email marketing campaigns, revamping its targeting and messages based on feedback to achieve much higher click-through rates. That success created another source of data it could then leverage to solve a follow-on problem: customers opting out of communications after receiving what they perceived to be too many emails from the company. It developed algorithms to predict how many times a customer could be offered another product or service before they opted out of email communication. The same is true for any organization; as it goes down the path, occasionally it will reassess by checking where it is, how conditions might have shifted. It should perennially revisit how its chosen initiatives are and should be structured and sequenced.

Drawing the Road Map: What's the Path to the Greatest Success?

With an assortment of valuable opportunities identified and a good sense of your organization's automation maturity, it becomes possible to lay out the road map—or blueprint, if you prefer—that visualizes the journey from today's position to some date in the future (see Figure 4.3). Which project should we do first, and at what pace should we try to go? The road map would also suggest the pace, tracks, and deployment strategies

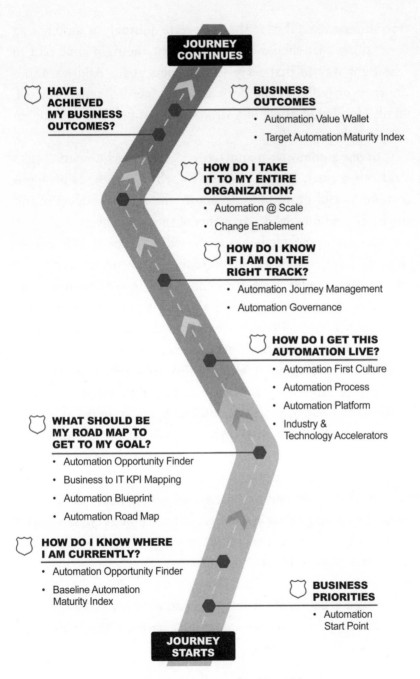

FIGURE 4.3   **Automation Road Map**

for automation. This is the long-term journey of automating everything that should be automated at the right time and in the right way to best serve the business goals. And it's also a journey of building the deep expertise needed across new IT skills, developing these in a structured manner, and creating an automation-first culture.

In one automotive manufacturer's case, the automation map laid out a clear, logical journey by which hundreds of applications would be introduced across the sales, production and logistics, and finance departments of the company.

Be sure to include how success will be tracked. It is important to have established the baseline at the outset to be able to measure the ROI on automation. In this company's case, knowing the baseline up front allowed it to point to dramatic results, such as a 20 percent reduction in customer complaints, an automated application management solution that yielded a 50 percent reduction in resolution time to customer complaints, and a huge drop in CIO-level escalation of problems, thanks to better development processes and intelligent automation.

Sketch out the journey map on two levels: the progress to business results and the progress to greater automation maturity in the organization. Both lines of progress need to be informed and well thought out as a series of quick wins followed by subsequent opportunities across various processes, tools, and technologies. The business results journey is typically structured as a three-phase process:

Phase 1. Establish: Assess automation potential and identify pilot processes across the enterprise for specific applications/solutions.

Phase 2. Scale: Develop, deploy, and scale solutions.

Phase 3. Operate: Extend geographic coverage for full value realization, revisit longer-term automation strategy based on learnings.

Meanwhile, the road map should also plan the automation journey as a series of steps moving from where a company is on the maturity index to higher levels of automation maturity in the future. If it's a "three," the map should anticipate the steps to becoming a "four." This should present a path from today's as-is automation environment to the to-be environment envisioned some years in the future.

A design thinking workshop or other form of collaborative brainstorming session can be a very useful part of creating an automation road map or blueprint. The term *design thinking* refers to a kind of movement in management thinking by which modern principles of industrial engineering, like design for usability, have been translated from the realm of sleek products like handheld devices and kitchen appliances, to other aspects of business competition, such as customer interfaces and business models.

Faced with whatever kind of problem, design thinking begins with a human-centered approach and aims to arrive at innovative solutions by setting aside limiting assumptions based on how a problem has been solved in the past. By following a sound design thinking methodology, a workshop can effectively set a positive, creative tone and provide a big-thinking, value-focused arena to imagine and explore opportunities. Design thinking facilitation can increase people's focus on business outcomes rather than technological hurdles, emphasize opportunities rather than shortcomings, and encourage a willingness to innovate and celebrate innovation culture rather than stick to a seemingly less risky status quo.

Having an automation road map is extremely useful to a CIO, given that executive's broad responsibility to apply IT to achieve organizational goals. From a CIO lens, an enterprise is divided into multiple organizations, such as lines of business, projects, run support, infrastructure, digital, security, and so on. Automation has to be scaled across all these areas. It requires a comprehensive road map to manage this complexity and drive automation at speed and scale. It makes an organization more able to drive automation holistically.

In the past few years, we have seen companies apply automation in pieces, using, say, virtual agents for customer service, human resource bots, and predictive models in other areas. To unleash the full potential of automation, it is important to apply automation across the organization and with an enterprise-level perspective.

Study, Strategize, Solve

The emphasis at the beginning of this chapter on choosing spots carefully and not investing in a patchwork quilt of unconnected areas does not necessarily mean that fewer total automation projects will be undertaken. In fact, having a rational way to choose initiatives paves the way for more projects in the long run.

We see leaders adopting high-impact solutions earlier, reinvesting more frequently based on the returns they produce, and acquiring technology in a way that is both accelerated and more deliberate. For example, when the automotive manufacturer cited earlier set priorities for its intelligent automation efforts, it soon became clear—in light of its goal to dramatically reduce production stoppages—that many parts of its operations could be part of the solution and were candidates for automation at some level. Ultimately, their automation road map covered hundreds of applications, ranging across many areas of sales and finance, as well as the expected production and logistics operations.

The key is to study, strategize, and solve. How should a team go about finding and assessing automation opportunities? It should start with gathering inputs and as much information as possible about existing processes, systems, and data. Then get clear on overall business priorities. Then study, strategize, and solve—that is, the team should generate insights from data analytics and benchmarking that point to good automation opportunities. Strategize which of those opportunities to prioritize based on their business impact; then design specific automation solutions in line with the organization's capacities for developing and embracing new technologies (see Figure 4.4).

Study

Study the as-is automation environment and identify opportunities. Here the question is: What are the possibilities? For this, use the automation opportunity finding approach, involving assessment and analytics, to identify areas where automation could have major impact on productivity or enable new value production and growth by leveraging people's talents. Use the maturity model to gauge the organization's current capacity to develop sophisticated solutions. The output is a set of business-centric automation ideas.

Strategize

Design the to-be automation environment and prioritize the opportunities. Here the question is: Which opportunities are we best positioned to exploit? For this, use the road map exercise, utilizing brainstorming/design thinking workshops to understand

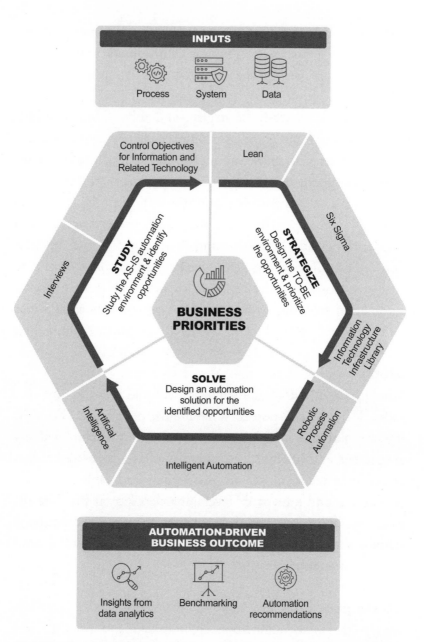

FIGURE 4.4   **Identifying and Assessing Automation Opportunities**

business objectives and to plot out the best series of steps to achieve them. Decisions are made here on what to automate and how.

Solve

Devise an automation solution for the identified opportunity. Here the question is: How do we execute most effectively on our plan? The goal is to develop and deploy solutions, as specified by the road map, efficiently and to high quality standards.

Conclusion

This chapter was designed to address the question facing every major company today: What should we automate to have the most positive impact on business performance? Companies need a rigorous process for focusing their organizations on the automation initiatives that matter most and doing them in the right order.

Yes, there is something to be said for spontaneous experimentation and "letting a thousand flowers bloom" in the form of scattered automation projects. Not everything has to fit into a preordained strategy.

Look at the way a sense of experimentation helped Domino's Pizza in its successful recent transformation. The company acknowledges it took a risk when it introduced voice ordering on its app some years ago. But as CEO J. Patrick Doyle explained, it was worth it: "We fundamentally believe that voice is a far more effective and efficient way for people to interact with technology. . . . What we do with it is going to be refined over time, but we need to get into this and start learning."[4]

Imagine an electrician who installs a new gadget for a customer, such as a video doorbell. If she doesn't figure out a way to integrate it with other devices in the house, like the security system or the family's cell phones, it won't be possible to achieve the benefits of a truly connected home.

A similar scenario plays out on a much grander scale across global organizations. CIOs, CDOs, and CEOs understand technology's significance to their company's strategy and growth. So in every industry, they're adopting technology that spawns new capabilities. Despite these substantial investments, many still struggle to transfer innovations across the enterprise and realize their potential. Often following fads, they put in place technologies as individual point solutions without a vision for how technologies will complement each other and without a plan for cultivating enterprise systems. As a result, when a potentially game-changing innovation comes along, they cannot effectively scale it.

To avoid that problem, it is best to start with a three-part effort to eradicate, optimize, and automate. First, eliminate unnecessary work by eradicating issues and inefficiencies permanently through root cause analysis. Then optimize the effort required to perform recurring tasks by bringing in assets and tools. And only then proceed with the intelligent automation of the activities—partially or fully, depending on priorities in the whole cycle of work. *Eradicate* the issues and inefficiencies permanently by resolving the root cause of frequently occurring issues. A typical outcome is reduced incidents. *Optimize* the effort required to perform recurring tasks by bringing in assets and tools. A typical outcome is faster process execution. And fully or partially *automate* the life-cycle activities using intelligent automation and AI to drive productivity improvement.

Ampol's Intelligent Automation Journey

Ampol, Australia's leading transport fuels company, took a business-focused approach to automation, leveraging robotic process automation in combination with optical character recognition, AI, and other forms of intelligent automation to automate business processes across the enterprise.

Although business process automation is often touted as a cost-out alternative to human labor, Ampol found significant value in reengineering processes to take advantage of these technologies to do things that were simply not feasible with its human workforce. These include:

- Replicating its pricing in real time across multiple systems with 100 percent accuracy
- Taking on carrier scheduling for large new customers well in excess of the capacity of its human labor force
- Implementing fraud-monitoring detection on a 24/7 basis

The automation practice uses Agile test and learn processes for each automation to determine its appropriateness and readiness to be automated. It then implements the reengineered automated process in a managed way. This involves the technology being treated as an intern employee by the human team for a period of time to ensure it is working effectively, before being released to run autonomously. This approach has led to a high success rate with automations and genuine, measurable value realization.

The bot farm is managed by an intelligent automation layer. Robotic automated processes are notoriously fragile and susceptible to failure due to any minor change in the surrounding landscape. The intelligent automation layer monitors the farm continuously, helping with the operation of the bots and monitoring for process errors, and performing self-healing operations for common errors where there is a known resolution.

Machine learning algorithms predict the run time of processes, both allowing more efficient scheduling to be performed and abnormal run times to be alerted for investigation. Errors are trapped and screen shots taken automatically to enable support resolution, or to identify scripting uplifts to handle less-common scenarios and to build resilience into the processing. These measures have led to a significant increase in the resilience and reliability of the bots, with a reduction in process failures requiring human intervention of over 40 percent.

Looking forward, Ampol anticipates that it will extend its use of intelligent automation across its entire technology landscape, leveraging the monitoring and self-healing capabilities already developed and utilizing blockchain to prevent tampering, to improve availability and efficiency of its IT operations. This will increase availability of business services and significantly reduce the cost of maintenance and build activities.

Key Takeaways

▶ So many opportunities exist for applying intelligent automation that an organization must have a rational, ongoing way to choose its spots.

▶ The best "next project" to tackle will be one located at the intersection of an organization's priorities and its preparedness—what solutions it needs most and what solutions it is most capable of implementing.

▶ What problem matters most to the business? The answer comes from ROI analysis that factors in not only cost savings but also top-line gains.

▶ What problem is our intelligent automation talent prepared to address? To know this, an organization should construct and track progress on an intelligent automation maturity model.

5

Plan the Plan

After strategic choices have been made and laid out and a journey map for how they will unfold is created, it is understandable that an automation team will want to move quickly into execution mode. There is, however, a crucial step that it should not neglect. The team needs to develop a plan that encompasses its whole portfolio of projects and to think through all the basic elements that must be in place for all the automation initiatives to succeed. Ultimately, the entire automation effort adds up to more than the sum of its parts.

This is where the idea of an automation operating model comes into play. Many readers will have heard the term *operating model* and it can be confusing, so let's simplify what it refers to: an operating model is just an organized template for how work gets accomplished in a high-quality way, over and over again. It identifies all the elements that should be established, well managed, and working in concert if the ambition is to have an ongoing capability in some area rather than a onetime success with a single initiative.

The key to successful operation and governance of intelligent automation largely depends on active participation from business leaders. Having an operating model for automation assumes that the intent is not just to knock out a few isolated automation pilots and point solutions, but rather that there will be multiple, perhaps numerous, different projects. Investing the time and energy to outline a model for operating recognizes that there are benefits to be gained by approaching them in a consistent way and allowing them to draw on a set of shared foundational resources.

A simple example of one element in an operating model is having an integrated model across the business units, different organizational entities, and ecosystem partners. Does it make sense to have a hundred different project teams figuring out how to align to the business models, structure projects, and come to terms on performance metrics within the same organization or with the same set of vendors? This aspect of the work is much better done in the same way across the enterprise. Better yet, it can be managed by a dedicated function or organization that not only has focused expertise and current knowledge of business priorities and organization models, but also can use the combined needs of all the projects it represents to strike more favorable terms and form more productive, collaborative business unit/partner relationships. Meanwhile, project teams relieved of that task are better able to focus their own energies and time on solution development and deployment.

There are many ways in which automation projects can make repeated use of sound approaches and tools. But surprisingly, establishing an operating model is probably the most neglected part of organizations' automation journeys. This chapter offers a strong starting point for developing an operating model. Without making all the decisions for our readers—which will necessarily depend on their circumstances—we outline the questions that need to be asked and offer a generic diagram of all the elements that need to be put in place.

A Holistic View

Every individual automation project should have its own well-thought-out plan, of course, but the organizations we know that have already enjoyed some initial successes with tactical solutions recognize that they should manage their efforts at a higher, collective level. Even after just a few automation projects are undertaken, it quickly becomes clear that these projects tend to interconnect and overlap—both in the business problems they are targeting and the implementation issues they are encountering. If an organization lacks a cohesive approach, often the same "wheels" are reinvented—in the form of answers to people, process, and technology issues—over and over again.

There are two possible ways of proceeding when projects have overlapping elements. Managers can address the same questions separately every time they come up, and have different automation project teams making their own decisions. Or they can carve out the issues faced in most automation projects from the issues that are unique for each project, and try to find robust answers that can work for all the project teams. Choosing this latter approach is essentially the same as saying, "Let's create an operating model."

The benefits of the operating model approach are clear. For the project teams working on solutions, it takes a tremendous amount of work off their plates. No one finds it fulfilling to spend months on questions that have already been answered elsewhere, even if they all arrive at the same great arrangements—which they usually do not. Being able to leverage work already done on this shared set of project management concerns allows teams to proceed in a light and agile way on their own highly focused solution developments and deployments.

Across the enterprise, any element taken off teams' plates means multiples of time saved and costs avoided. More than that, it means much more potential for efforts in one corner of the organization to advance work in other corners. Synergies as well as economies of scale are the great benefits of a well-constructed operating model.

Constructing a Framework

What does an operating model look like? Typically, it is drawn as a set of boxes, or modules, arranged side-by-side and in stacks to indicate the relationships between the different elements. Rather than a simple list of areas to think about, it is a framework for comprehending the overall structure of a well-managed environment.

Within the realm of enterprise IT systems, an early example of a generic operating model was a framework developed over a decade ago by Jay Ramanathan and Rajiv Ramnath of The Ohio State University.[1] It was designed to show all that goes into building an IT group capable of delivering high-quality solutions to its internal customers. As well as the right set of capabilities in the staff, it called for management strengths in process design, governance, and performance management—and a sufficiently powerful technical stack. Combining these elements into a logical diagram made it easier to maintain managers' attention on all the essential parts—and made the point that weakness in any of these areas could hobble the IT group's ability to deliver.

Since then, organizations have created many variations on the framework, according to their own needs. Figure 5.1 shows the diagram used by one company we know to outline its automation operating model. Presenting the big picture of automation in this way is useful for assessing the sophistication of a given organization's automation capabilities and targeting areas for improvement.

BUSINESS UNIT				
Opportunity Identification			Benefit Realization & Tracking	
AUTOMATION STRATEGY	**INNOVATION & INCUBATION**	**DELIVERY & CHANGE MANAGEMENT**	**AUTOMATION OPERATIONS**	**TECHNOLOGIES & PLATFORMS**
Automation Strategy	Innovation Management	Agile Project Management	Automation Monitoring & Scheduling	Infrastructure/ Cloud Automation
	Prototyping	Automation Change Management	Technology Operations	RPA/Chatbots
Sourcing Strategy		Automation Development	Service Operations	Business Process Management
Governance & Controls		Automation Deployment	Security Management	Data & Analytics
				Application Automation
	AUTOMATION ENABLERS			
Portfolio & Demand Management	Data & Information Management	Workforce & Talent Management		Internet of Things
	Asset & Knowledge Management	Resilience & Business Continuity		Automation Architecture
Legal & Compliance	**CENTRALIZED MANAGEMENT**			Future Technologies
	Partner & Alliance Management			

FIGURE 5.1 Sample Automation Operating Model

Glancing at the figure above, it is clear that there are many areas requiring focused thinking and decision-making. At the headline level, they include how the automation team should approach:

- ▸ Opportunity identification
- ▸ Benefit realization and tracking
- ▸ Automation strategy
- ▸ Innovation and incubation
- ▸ Delivery and change management
- ▸ Automation operations
- ▸ Technologies and platforms
- ▸ Automation enablers
- ▸ Centralized and partner/alliance management

Within most of these are multiple subcategories to address as well. Again, note that these are not simply presented as a list of concerns. The placement of these areas relative to each other also conveys relationships among them, with certain cross-cutting activities supporting groups of others. Let's start at the top of the model, with the business-unit-relevant concerns of opportunity identification and benefit realization and tracking. Why are these at the top? Because they are the paramount concerns from which everything below must follow. All automation project teams must be driven by the search for high-value opportunities and be able to track their success in delivering that value to the business.

Opportunity Identification

This essential starting point for intelligent automation has already been discussed at length; it is the whole focus of Chapter 4. Part of a company's operating model should be exactly that kind of codification of how opportunity assessment gets done. Tools like the automation assessment tool and the automation maturity model are powerful aids to this process, so the model might identify them as tools every project team should use. Individual projects should not need to reinvent this fundamental process of translating the strategic intent of the business into specific automation initiatives with high potential to provide a competitive automation edge.

Benefit Realization and Tracking

Neither should every team be coming up with its own methodology for addressing that overriding concern: How will our success be gauged? How will we know if our intelligent automation is on track and yielding the projected payoffs? To answer questions like these a company must establish what it will measure and how. In the parlance of management, it needs to spell out key performance indicators, or KPIs.

There are various methods for doing this in a consistent way. The "goal, question, metric," or GQM, approach is one option that is commonly used in large organizations to attach useful metrics to their software processes. First named by David Weiss, it has been championed by Victor Basili of the University of Maryland, College Park.[2] Another effective approach is the one VeriSM uses to establish quantifiable measures within its broad service management framework for businesses undergoing digital transformations.[3]

Of course, the specific goals of different projects will lead them to different particular metrics—all defined by the business value goals. So, for example, if a service organization wants to reduce its customer complaints by 50 percent, it would need to determine which applications were affected by this. What was the number of complaints before a solution was implemented? Does the organization's system accurately capture the number of customer complaints? The same kind of thinking would be applied to a ticket management process in an IT services group.

In each case, there must be a measurement framework established up front so that once the solution is in its implementation stage, it can accurately report what is happening on a real-time basis.

Given the great variety of metrics that will be used by individual automation projects, the point of this part of the operating model is to equip project teams with a proven way of arriving at them. It is also a reminder that this is an essential part of a sustainable automation environment.

Too many managers, full of enthusiasm for the productivity and other benefits they expect to flow from an automation project, fail at the outset to set out clearly how those benefits will be measured and monitored—and for that matter, in what forms they will come. Measuring project-level ROI is important not only as feedback to ongoing decision-making but also to win additional funding.

Within Accenture, we find it most compelling to do this in bottom-line financial terms. When someone applies AI to solve a problem, they have to deposit the value they project it will generate over a given time frame. That is treated as a debit. As the implementation progresses, they then track how those business benefits are materializing, and that allows them to take out the money they put in. Once they cross the deposit threshold, they can start claiming an ROI on that AI investment and tracking the return as it rises.

Finally, a message that must always be reinforced is that KPIs should get to the heart of what really matters to success. Often, project managers gravitate to measures that are objective and easily quantifiable—but the mere fact that a measure is easier to track doesn't mean it is a better one. Always remember that automation is not just about cost take-out. Other goals might include error reduction, having people shift to higher value-add activities, improving the customer experience, or bringing innovations to market faster, any of which could have metrics assigned to them.

It's important to identify all the measures that matter—the most salient metrics based on the business objectives—and outline a standard method for reporting on them. Take the case of an online retailer, for example. There are many aspects of performance it can choose to capture and monitor to know if its customer experience, sales volumes, and profit margins are heading in the right direction. Typical metrics include average customer time required to place an order and elapsed time from order to delivery, frequency of shopping cart abandonment, and volume of sales that can be attributed to real-time product recommendations.

As consumers, we all see how the feedback from such measurement leads to adjustments. Online storefronts are constantly tweaked based on what is found to work better or worse, down to the littlest details of site navigation, color palette, text fonts, icon designs, and the size and shape of "Add to Cart" and "Buy Now" buttons. Experiments are deployed daily to test hunches about what might make it easier for customers to initiate and complete transactions. Analytics engines used to serve up next-purchase recommendations are continually updated with fresh data regarding individual customers' searches, past purchasing, and posted feedback—as well as broad patterns revealed across all customers of how interest in, say, a film or piece of music, correlates with interest in other available products.

Such targeted marketing is only possible in highly data-driven environments. The takeaway is that any company can improve only what it accurately measures. So it must establish what measures matter most to business success, how to track them tightly, and how to ensure the tracking translates to value-creating adjustments.

Automation Strategy

Chapter 3 laid out the importance of thinking strategically about automation. While we rarely think of devising strategy as an infrastructural layer of work, it is clearly another realm in which individual projects should be able to benefit from cross-enterprise groundwork. As shown in Figure 5.1, this part of the operating model is about providing teams with more than strategy for automation per se—rather it involves the design and updating of the automation road map and imposition of standards and policies. It also calls for cross-enterprise guidance on sourcing strategy—including how to make decisions on whether to build or buy—and sound approaches to portfolio and demand management.

Legal and compliance matters also crop up in virtually every project and should be addressed consistently within a coherent enterprisewide framework for security and risk management. How does intelligent automation associated risk get flagged and mitigated, for example? As one executive in a global healthcare services company notes, "more technology creates huge upside in healthcare, but it also brings risk. So, one thing I see changing is cybersecurity and privacy considerations in every place we deploy technology in healthcare."[4] Risk management considerations have to be part of planning the plan—not something to wait and deal with after a crisis occurs.

Perhaps most important, the operating model should provide for consistent governance of automation projects—especially to the degree that automation is seen as a key lever in business transformation. The key questions here are: What kinds of decisions do projects often find they must answer in progress? How can we ensure that these will, as a matter of course, be made in a way that considers varying perspectives but still delivers timely answers? Who should be part of making them and what roles will they play in the process?

One company we know is especially thoughtful about automation governance and how to involve sufficient representation of top management in driving decisions and monitoring impact. It created a steering committee, decided who should be on it, and specified how they would use certain tools to track what was going on. Establishing such oversight has maintained coherence, even as it has scaled its automation initiatives dramatically and empowered more and more teams to identify and pursue opportunities.

The involvement of top management has resulted in other benefits, too. While some business unit managers had previously given little attention to automation and regarded it as an optional activity, seeing some of their most senior colleagues involved in its governance drew their attention and led them to view automation as increasingly necessary.

By contrast, in companies without governance mechanisms in place, we have seen serious stumbles at the point that an automation solution seems ready to scale. Operational issues arose that no one was prepared to handle or make decisions about—a development that could have been avoided if good governance had flagged them as concerns earlier.

Good governance also oversees the rollout of projects over time according to some logic. For example, after an opportunity assessment has identified top candidates for automation projects, part of governance is to consider how, by addressing one of these use cases first, the path could be paved for other applications—either by putting a technological building block in place or by producing quick-win financial gains that could be used to fund a subsequent project. It is the proper work of a governance group to map out that kind of sequence, enforce it, and revise it if necessary, in response to unforeseen challenges and opportunities.

Innovation and Incubation

Not every intelligent automation project comes out of the gate with a strong business case, committed sponsor, and clear project plan established. Sometimes the potential seems to be high, but success depends on certain unknowns regarding the technologies involved or the acceptance of them by customers or users. This is why an automation operating model should also provide for experimentation and research purely in the name of innovation.

It should be possible, for example, to pilot a machine-learning solution that discovers new data associations. Afterward, the outcomes can be reviewed with an eye toward identifying new opportunities for growth and innovation, such as a new customer segment or creating a new product. There should be innovation management processes in place to take efforts from idea generation and screening through prototyping and incubation of new solutions or products. An enterprisewide commitment to automation innovation should also provide for maintaining a library of reusable building blocks for automation projects.

When a large multinational energy company asked us for a single-line diagnosis of what they were dealing with in 2017, we helped them determine that innovation and speed to market were most important. That year, the company's IT function was challenged to reduce effort by more than 60 percent using automation and reduce operating costs by between 50 percent and 60 percent, while also increasing the average speed of its software solution delivery.

Managers ran a series of workshops and hackathons to generate ideas and identify and prioritize areas using an opportunity assessment process. The IT group, while it was still in the midst of its automation journey, had already saved millions of dollars and redeployed staff amounting to nearly 100 full-time

equivalents (FTEs), while at the same time speeding up operations and improving reliability. Managers were convinced that
the IT group successes owed a lot to the centralized automation
framework and platform it set up for the entire automation ecosystem and its provision for investing in innovation.

So far, most other companies have been devoting their whole
budgets to creating solutions. We haven't seen many companies
allocating parts of their budgets to the meta level of automation
thinking. Only recently have such innovation funds begun to
show up in leading organizations' budgets.

It is true that unless an organization sees automation as integral to its strategic intent, it does not devote separate funding to
staying abreast of new developments and devising small-scoped
efforts to try out new tools. But having a top-down strategic
commitment to intelligent automation and data science means
providing for research and development investment and specifically innovation-oriented programs. The funds can be used
to explore especially promising automation initiatives. This is
budgeting at the level of strategic initiatives and it is part of
encouraging more managers and staff to think at that level.

Delivery and Change Management

What else does it take to move an application of intelligent
automation from successful proof of concept to use at industrial scale? Much of what an operating model includes helps
answer this question. Project teams are often built for solutions
development—but business impact relies on solutions delivery and the attention to change management that makes it go
smoothly.

Under this category, we see operating models specifying best practices for project teams to approach Agile project
management, automation change management, automation

development, and automation deployment. They equip teams to oversee committed portfolios of automation projects to meet business needs; to iteratively design, develop, test, and roll out automation solutions; and to do life-cycle management of enterprise applications.

Much of this is a matter of institutionalizing and industrializing sound software practices. At the end of the day, an intelligent automation solution is made up of software. The same DevOps leading practices that are used in other critical systems should be applied to automation. Teams should test everything, monitor usage and changes, and measure and evaluate results. All the rules of software engineering apply. There should be methodology, there should be a process, there should be security considerations. Outlining and enforcing a common best way of running projects is the best way to avoid many headaches. Automation frameworks and processes should be established that are aligned to industry-proven standards like ITIL, CMMI, VeriSM, Six Sigma, and so forth.

Teams need to create the impact and transition plans required to scale their intelligent automation projects. Proper planning will enable a smooth transition, so that the workforce and processes can work well alongside the newly automated elements.

One topic worth calling out in more detail in this part of the operating model is *design authority*. Whether it's a role for a single individual or for a group of people bringing different perspectives to bear, the value of a design authority has been proven many times over in the realm of enterprise architecture. The job of the authority is to vet all solution designs in terms of whether they will accomplish what they are intended to do and whether they are well enough aligned with the broader architecture to pose no integration problems.

To do this job well over time, the design authority must create and enforce a variety of standards for architecture and design, relating to what frameworks and methodologies should be followed, how processes should be outlined, and what tools should be favored. This may sound like introducing an extra layer of bureaucracy, but in practice, establishing appropriate authority over such matters enables faster and more effective change. Especially where a design authority operates in a collaborative design thinking environment, it can ensure coherent, consistent, and customer-centric automation applications that deliver real business value.

Automation Operations

Various tools to help in automation operations should be supplied to teams, and they should be trained in their use as part of the standard operating model. All of them, for example, need to schedule and monitor their pipelines and track the evolution of models and data sets using metrics. Effective ways to do automation monitoring and scheduling should be extended across the enterprise, not reinvented in its various corners. The same goes for technology operations, service operations, and security management.

The operating model can outline how to manage day-to-day automation operations and provide business and technical support; how to monitor, measure, report, and review current performance; and how to optimize automation scheduling and maintain an integrated view of schedule dependencies with interacting applications.

Technology and Platforms

Any large-scale automation environment demands a depth of knowledge surrounding a great variety of technologies and platforms. To name just the major ones, they fall into the following categories:

- ▸ Infrastructure/cloud automation
- ▸ Robotic process automation/chatbots
- ▸ Business process management
- ▸ Data and analytics
- ▸ Application automation
- ▸ Internet of Things/Industrial Internet of Things
- ▸ Automation architecture
- ▸ Future technologies

The key questions here are: What other elements are required to make sure that the solutions and systems put in place are adaptive and flexible? How will it be clear that new efforts are required to update a solution? For example, we often find that the leaders in enterprise applications, before launching intelligent automation solutions, set up complementary technologies such as data lakes (a system or repository of data stored in its raw format) and cloud services (any service made available to users on demand via a cloud computing provider's servers).

Applications automations are available in every shape and size: anyone looking for testing tools in the market, for example, will find a lot of them. With apps being built every day by a whole host of AI and technology startups, the wealth of choices just from an automation perspective itself can seem overwhelming. Within any given large organization, we typically find some 10 to 15 different testing tools in use.

So how does a company make it simple? This is the job of an operating model, which sticks to what is very contextual to the organization. Different organizations can have very dissimilar environments, even if they are in the same sector and at the same maturity level. Here, as elsewhere in the operating model, design has to match what is right for the organization with its priorities and even values. Managers should start with understanding where it is today, where they want it to go, and what makes sense in terms of a journey map—again, very aligned to the specific organization.

Automation Enablers

Under this category come principles and practices for data and information management, workforce and talent management, asset and knowledge management, and resilience and business continuity. All these are shared, foundational capabilities that enable automation efforts to succeed if they are well established in advance.

Data is one of the biggest enablers of success that must be addressed in a comprehensive and coherent way. In the context of any individual automation project, data scientists must confirm that the data sets are complete and accurate and that the algorithms are appropriate. They run up against a wall if the organization as a whole has not made data management a priority.

Also fundamental to automation is the capture of the knowledge and experience that has been applied in the past on a repetitive task or problem. This is why reusability is such a key concept in driving automation benefits across an enterprise. Automation leaders establish libraries of reusable automation assets and knowledge and actively build them as their enterprises gain experience and maturity in automation.

Workforce and talent management is another competence that must be established on an enterprisewide basis. The operating model should address how workers will be appropriately trained and enabled. Across projects there will be many commonalities in the new skills needed to do automation. Someone needs to be asking at a high level: What kind of technology skills should we have? And someone must plan for the necessary training and create the enablement materials to allow people to do their roles effectively. Should training be video-based, delivered online, in the form of short training modules? Many aspects of the training approach deserve careful attention. Without an operating model, it is too much to expect that solution teams will have a vision and plan for doing training effectively, let alone that they will be able to set up training as a continuous activity.

Centralized and Partner/Alliance Management

In the chapter we devoted to strategy, we discussed establishing an ecosystem with partner or vendor networks. So partner and alliance management are a point of consideration in the operating model. It is possibly the easiest case of all to be made for managing automation on an enterprisewide basis. It requires up-to-date knowledge of an extremely dynamic group of external solution providers, which can only be maintained by dedicating resources to scanning the ecosystem partner space. There is also a body of knowledge that is quite specialized relating to service-level agreements, how they are structured, and how they are enforced.

A good operating model includes guidelines on managing relationships with existing partners, systems integration partners, and internal IT departments. It offers proven ways to verify and review the performance against agreed commitments and push for improvements when needed.

All Together Now

If all these elements are planned at a level above the individual automation project, what a company has is a more holistic approach to investing in and scaling automation across the enterprise. It has the ability to manage automation at a total organization level and a solid foundation for every new opportunity in intelligent automation to get traction and succeed. It has an operating model—a management framework that sits below the level of overall strategic goals for automation and above the level of managing the detailed work of supporting particular business operations and solving particular operational challenges. Think of the operating model as the essential link from strategic intent to execution. It shines a light on all the areas that must be well managed for an organization to claim an automation edge and shares decisions made within each of these areas.

One way to think of it is that organizations that are venturing into the space of automation, AI, and digitization need to progress through three steps: study, strategize, and solve. The first part, *study*, is the automation opportunity finding we discussed in Chapter 4—the analytics-based approach that identifies the art of possibility to guide automation investments. The last part, *solve*, is the creation of the specific solutions identified. But in between is a critical *strategize* part. This consists of creating the road map. It often involves brainstorming and design thinking workshops to ensure that solutions will map to the company's capabilities and business objectives. And it involves creating an operating model.

An operating model is vital because it translates an automation strategy into a robust framework within which individual business solutions can be efficiently planned and coordinated. It takes what could otherwise be a chaotic environment and makes it clear and discussable by an organization's top leadership, line managers, and many operational teams. A well-established operating model:

- ▸ Provides the means by which the automation strategy is translated into operating results
- ▸ Provides a clear, consensus-driven guide for the delivery of solutions
- ▸ Ensures faster revenue growth and higher operating margins

In short, how an automation initiative starts matters. An organization will succeed better in the end with all its automation efforts if it has an execution plan that is well aligned with a high-level vision for enterprise competitiveness. But as it starts, so should it continue: an operating model also needs to be a living model, constantly subjected to scrutiny, and revised in light of new developments.

As-Is Versus To-Be

We have been discussing an operating model as a necessary element in an automation transformation, and perhaps creating the impression that any operating model is better than none at all. That is not necessarily true. In the same way that a business process can be known and consistently followed but still far from optimal in its efficiency or effectiveness, so can an operating model leave much to be desired. One of the great benefits of diagramming an operating model is to support productive conversations among different parties in an organization about how things are done—and how they could be done better.

Different organizations will go at different paces, according to their maturity level and adoption of automation so far. Wholly depending on business priorities, organizational readiness, and technology readiness, an enterprise has to decide how to drive automation forward, achieving quick wins with, say, robotic process automation applications, while also refining at this higher level how it manages project sequencing, ensures alignment to business priorities, enables speedier implementations, manages risks, and so forth.

The as-is form of the operating model may fall short in various respects, but those failings may go undiagnosed without a clear picture of it on which to focus. Reviewing the as-is model and finding its weakest spots can point the way to a better to-be operating model for the future. Then work can begin to improve it.

The Case for a Center of Excellence

Let's say a management team is now committed to putting in the effort to define an automation operating model. It may be asking, "Who oversees all this work? And how do they add value?" There are two basic choices on the *who* question: leave it to the business units who need automation solutions or create a centralized automation center of excellence (COE). Which of these, for a given company, will be the more effective structure?

Increasingly, we see companies opting for a COE model as their preferred way of achieving synergies and consistencies through education and scaling support—while also encouraging initiative and experimentation at the business unit level. Our observation is supported by more formal research by others. For example, in a 2019 *Forbes* survey of over 300 executives familiar with their companies' intelligent automation efforts, the majority (51 percent) responded that they had either already established a COE or "digital management office" and another 41 percent said they were planning to do so.[5]

One additional consideration makes us believe that organizations will continue to gravitate toward setting up COEs: they are inherently more capable of self-improvement and evolution over time. Like all parts of the organization, a COE can be thought of as more or less mature relative to its equivalents in other large enterprises.

It is simply easier for a dedicated COE to develop self-awareness of its current state of maturity and a sense of resolve to keep improving. Critical, of course, are leadership and sponsorship. These are essential to setting direction and establishing controls, defining an automation strategy, creating frameworks for innovation and incubation, and establishing governance and controls. Figure 5.2 offers a simple maturity model for an automation COE that can help guide a maturity assessment and provide a snapshot of all the capabilities a center of excellence must evolve over time. It should constantly build its capacities for:

- **Business functions contributing as major stakeholders to the IT organization.** Having one central group focusing on business-IT alignment ensures that solutions stay closest to customers and are effectively delivered through IT. A COE can track customer expectations, align them to business priorities and to IT, and work with IT on customer feedback.
- **IT organization alignment with the business.** There should be consistency in delivery management, disseminating best practices in discovery, and how teams design, test and deploy, configure, and support solutions.
- **Talent management.** A central group can look across the whole talent portfolio, while also gaining a high-level view of what works in change management, competency management, and assembling the hybrid workforce.

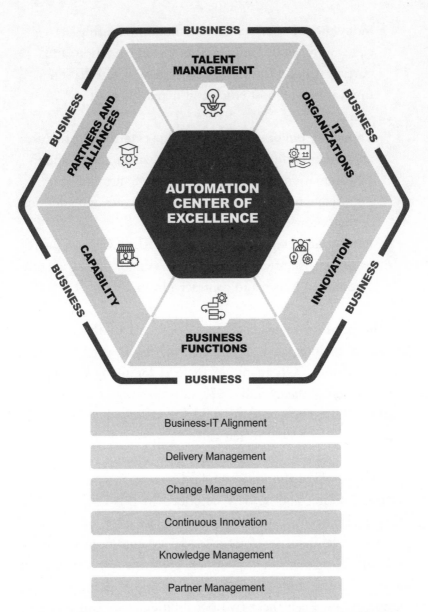

FIGURE 5.2 Automation Center of Excellence Maturity Model

▸ **Innovation.** Investments in maintaining leading-edge awareness, improving innovation execution, and participating in the vibrant ecosystem of automation innovation are most efficient if managed at an enterprise level.

▸ **Capability building and knowledge retention.** Structures and processes for knowledge management can maintain an automation knowledge hub, harvest automation knowledge from initiatives, and aid transfer and adoption of that knowledge.

▸ **Partner and alliance management.** The COE can focus on and constantly refine aspects of vendor management, automation usage, and contract administration.

The need to manage all these elements of the operating model in an integrated way is a strong argument for putting an automation COE in place. In fact, for many people, the terms *operating model* and *COE* seem synonymous. But it is possible to have an operating model in the absence of a COE. A decentralized model (often called a *federated* organizational model) provides for the same sharing of leading practices and other forms of collaborative standard setting, but pushes all the decision-making and activity described in this chapter to the individual business units. This is often termed a *community of practice* model because it brings together a community of managers all facing the same questions, gives them a platform for communicating and collaborating, but leaves them with full autonomy. Between these two possibilities, there can also be a hybrid approach, which centralizes some aspects of the operating model and decentralizes others. Let's look at them in a bit more detail.

Centralized Model

In a centralized model, all of the functions of a COE are performed by a single joint team of personnel from both the business and IT. This is the best-fit model for companies that are just establishing their automation capabilities. This works well in a scenario where a shared services model is highly centralized and where the automation opportunities are modest. This model is the one that facilitates movement from individualized to industrialized capability and sets the stage for implementation at scale.

Yes, there are some drawbacks with this model to note. With increasing scale of the organization, some groups' automations may be deprioritized, and some parts of the business may go into a silo and duplicate COE functions. In a centralized model, these tendencies must be recognized and addressed, and extra effort may have to go into evangelizing for automation programs.

Decentralized, Federated Model

If centralized teams can't fully drive and sustain automation across the organization, then they must succeed with a decentralized model. In this kind of model, they will tend to take much more tailored approaches to working with different parts of the business, while pursuing cross-cutting goals to embed deeper expertise in the organization and to compile and disseminate what is being learned in pockets of activity so it can inform other decisions and processes across the company.

By definition, this isn't really creating a center of excellence; it is creating multiple communities of practice. Information can certainly be shared among communities of practice to encourage standards and leverage common technology, but this model does bring redundancy and a higher cost for automation.

Hybrid Model

This model (see Figure 5.3) is a combination of centralization within a single small group where the standards are centralized, but the scalable automation execution engine capabilities are federated out among business units or as many groups as required.

The hybrid model works best when there is a large, globally distributed enterprise with highly decentralized decision-making. The automation COE may also contain an automation execution engine that interacts with business/customers, identifies opportunities, defines prioritizations, and provides automation delivery capabilities to business units. This works best for large, global organizations. The benefits of this model are faster industrialization, effective knowledge reuse, greater ease in scaling and in obtaining the required level of independent decision-making, and a stronger sense of ownership with the business units.

In summary, an automation COE is imperative for an organization's automation success. The model that organizations adopt should be driven by the organization's unique business model and the strategic direction. As long as the operating model is structured properly with clearly defined roles and responsibilities, either model should work to achieve the automation objectives.

In a sense, the COE is the steering committee that operates at the enterprise level to ensure consistent value realization. As one useful handbook for automation project steering committees outlines, effective project-level guidance focuses on five main tasks: making stop/continue decisions at various points in the project life cycle; reviewing and approving project financial projections; approving project timetables; ensuring that the design of the solution meets business requirements; and providing the

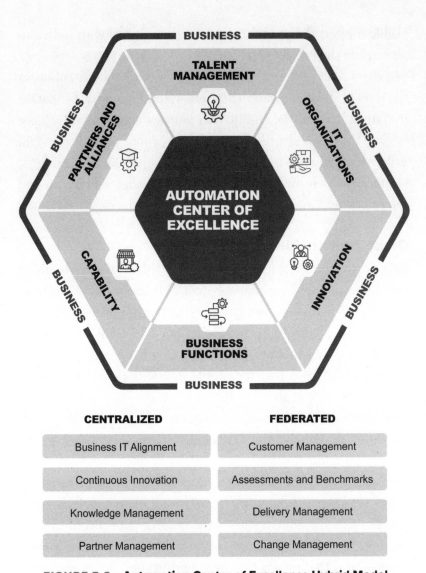

FIGURE 5.3   Automation Center of Excellence Hybrid Model

visible support the project manager needs to deal with individuals outside the project team.[6]

The COE performs an analogous governance function at the level of the organization's overall automation transformation initiative. It owns the automation journey and constantly asks: Is everything we identified as part of our journey still relevant, or has some change happened that has impacted the timing? It maintains a continuous focus on quality, value realization, and the importance of intelligent automation to the organization.

Diversity with Uniformity

Every organization features diversity that should be maintained and respected, and yet management also has to bring unity to that diversity. It can't simply force-fit what has been created for one part of the business to another part. It needs to be sensitive to how well solutions travel and to what extent they must be tweaked. This is true for people solutions as well as technological tools. For example, a payment-processing team might be very comfortable adopting a newly introduced technology, but the same technology might create disruption for another group. At a retail company we know, a chatbot quickly embraced by headquarters logistics staff seemed ideal to roll out to the truck-driver workforce. Among this group were many less tech-savvy people, so some adjustments were needed. The success of any chatbot depends on whether it can conduct a productive conversation—and that means that even within the same company, it might need to be equipped with a different vocabulary.

The biggest mistake that can be made in an operating model is to assume a false uniformity. Instead, it should allow for tailored customer journeys to be mapped out, according to whether groups within the organization are poised for fast-paced or slow-paced progress. A solution that assumes a three-month adoption time in one place may need to allow for a six-month adoption in another. A push to bring in process automation at scale may encounter pockets of software developers still early in their shift from traditional waterfall methodologies to the new age of Agile and DevOps.

Toward an Automation Platform

In the past, companies have aspired to introduce automation opportunistically, choosing spots here and there "where possible." Now, the understanding is growing that their approaches to automation should be holistic. This means that intelligent automation should be managed at an enterprise level, with a focus on the capabilities and standards that will be put in place to support many projects, and sequence them optimally. And it should be set up for scaling, which shifts the focus to whole-organization challenges: business readiness, data access and governance, culture and talent, platforms and architecture, and shifting to a platform mindset.

As briefly noted in an earlier chapter, recent years have seen the evolution of platform business models by which companies like Amazon enable third-party sellers of any size to tap into their large-scale infrastructures for flexible and reliable operational performance.

Managers responsible for building their organization's automation edge need to adopt that same mindset—that the biggest impact will come once they have created a platform that allows new ideas for automation to be turned into reality with minimum investment and then work seamlessly together. We expect to hear more automation experts talking about platformization as efforts to automate intensify.

This chapter has enabled a big step toward that vision by, we hope, inspiring automation managers to plan the plan—to lay out the details of how the overall effort will be organized and what all needs to be considered. In a nutshell we have tried to answer two questions: What would be valuable to have in place before a solution is developed, both to streamline its creation and to prepare its future users to make effective use of it? And how should those elements be put in place? The operating model components discussed here all pave the way for projects to move from proof of concept to industrial scale.

The following chapters continue to explore these essential elements in greater depth, but the point here is that these are the key considerations that any overall plan for high-impact automation should cover. Again, this is where a lot of organizations fail. They neglect to plan for and invest in building their automation capabilities at the enterprise level. By the same token, however, it represents a powerful opportunity to gain competitive advantage. One of the most important differentiators among industry peers and their performance in the years to come will come down to their relative dedication to putting an operating model in place—one that supports an increasingly digital workforce and a constant flow of simple, seamless, and sustainable automation solutions.

It sounds very basic, and it is. But do not underestimate how essential it is. Before a team can dive into the details of multilayered integration analysis, variant analysis, clustering, chatbots, and multiple robotic process automation applications, it must take time to plan the plan.

Key Takeaways

- To plan the plan is to take real care before diving into a project to architect how it will be staffed and conducted, who will govern its key decisions, and what metrics will be used to track its progress toward clear goals.
- Because planning the plan is a capability in itself, companies with ambitions to apply intelligent automation to problems in many areas should consider establishing an intelligent automation COE.
- Ideally, planning is done both at the project level and at a level above individual projects, so that part of the planning is to specify how synergies will be gained across these disparate efforts.

6

Architect for the Future

Constant disruption is now a given for businesses, affecting every part of today's commercial landscape. Companies cannot expect to put technology solutions in place and then simply move on, confident that the investment they made will continue on autopilot, spinning off value well into the future. Anything built today will inevitably be rendered obsolete tomorrow.

Yet most companies today are living with the legacy IT infrastructures and architectures built for a bygone era. Ultimately, the day must come when an organization faces the bigger-picture and longer-term challenge of overhauling the technology supporting the business. As projects proliferate, the cost of all those workarounds becomes unbearable; as the massive potential of intelligent automation starts to become clear, the opportunity for synergy becomes compelling. Surveys of business and IT leaders are beginning to reflect this new sense of priority: across the world, respondents cite architecture inflexibility as one of the biggest barriers to innovating at scale.

This chapter discusses how and why architecture is a critical element for the sustainability and scalability of enterprise automation. If an automation leader is well supported by a technical team and interested in more strategic and operational-level issues, they might choose to skip this chapter. Yet the discussion here is not terribly technical, being pitched instead at the level of highlighting the key technology considerations teams should keep in mind as they embark on building systems of enterprise automation that are resilient and scalable.

We look at some of the key architectural considerations for driving business benefits and to build automation that is faster-moving, adaptable to the ever-changing market, and aligned to the holistic organizational model (business process, modular data, infrastructure, and applications) that complements this evolution and enables greater flexibility. We look at the approaches of leaders who are ahead of the pack in their embrace of the principles that allow this evolution. And we describe the key considerations for supporting a scalable and sustainable automation journey in any organization.

Six Key Considerations

Enterprise automation architecture should be built with six key considerations:

- ▸ Systems must be *adaptive* to enable a business to quickly respond to dynamic markets. Achieve this with a plug-and-play architecture that can embrace technology changes, seamlessly integrate into a broader ecosystem of partners, and provide agility to the business.

▸ Establish a *data fabric* for intelligent automation and reap the benefits in business intelligence. Keep in mind that the point of the data fabric is not just to centralize enterprise data, but also to enrich it and maximize the use of data.

▸ Resolve from the outset to put *AI at the core* of the architecture. This is key to providing differentiated customer experiences for the business. An AI-infused automation architecture can self-learn, comprehend, adapt, and evolve to create new experiences for the customers.

▸ Move to the *cloud* for increased agility and greater cost-effectiveness in automation. At this point, cloud computing is becoming inevitable in the automation world. More and more companies are switching to cloud-based solutions.

▸ Architect for *security* to safeguard a company's intellectual property and customer privacy. Embed security into the architecture to maintain the confidentiality, integrity, and availability of sensitive information handled by applications.

▸ Adopt a *platform-centric* approach to integrate automation efforts and achieve synergies across the enterprise—and to support the industrializing and scaling of solutions.

Let's look at each of these key principles in a bit more depth (See Figure 6.1.)

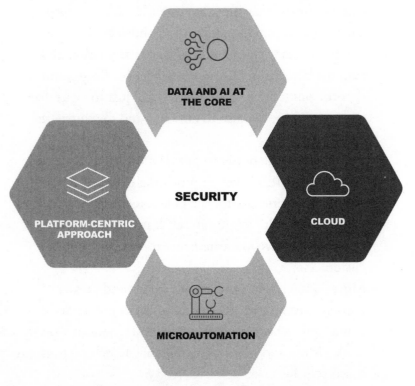

FIGURE 6.1 **Considerations for Building a Resilient Enterprise Automation Architecture**

Make It Adaptive

When intelligent automation is becoming the core of a business—driving transformations and augmenting business with powerful insights and decisions—it needs to quickly sense and respond to how the business is changing. Having a more adaptive architecture for automation enables the business to remove bottlenecks and barriers to change, ensure a smoothly flowing value chain, and continuously stay relevant to its customers. Moreover, many business strategies today are predicated on working through alliances and partnerships with other players in the market. Managers have long recognized partnering as a strategy to scale more quickly and to create more seamless end-to-end experiences for customers. If a business chooses to pursue this kind of strategy, however, it should have an automation architecture that can interface smoothly with the partner landscape—while still excelling, from the company's standpoint, as the central architecture and the hub around which all else revolves.

Think about the benefits of and the argument for an integrated automation approach across systems. No company starting out today would build its IT architecture to be otherwise. But again, this is the problem: in every company that exists today, an architecture is already in place. Very few companies have the clean-slate luxury to build for adaptivity across the board. Most are faced with the very big challenge of decoupling the elements of the existing technology stack that the automation solution will be executed upon.

The problem is not insurmountable, however. There are practical steps every company can take to move toward automation for integrated systems and to convert the challenge presented by the breakneck pace of technology into an opportunity to innovate and outperform the competition.

To build an adaptive intelligent automation, system architects can design automation technology to work in a distributed way, with every function that is required by an application set up separately from it and treated as an independent service provider to it. The benefit of approaching automation in this microservices-oriented way is that it allows those subfunctions—most of which play a significant supporting role and have always shared a great amount of commonality across applications—to be updated independently. Whenever there is some good reason to alter a function, the update process does not affect the rest of an application employing its service. And the same change can instantly benefit any other applications relying on that same function, with no disruption of their own performance.

If our explanation has been clear, it should be obvious how a microservices-based open architecture gives an enterprise a whole new plug-and-play capacity. Look at any large organization, and you see a highly diverse set of tools and technologies being used and rapidly evolving across the enterprise. If they are too entangled with interdependencies, this morass of applications becomes a barrier to introducing new elements; it just becomes too difficult to anticipate and deal with all their ripple effects across a densely connected system.

All this becomes especially important as a company moves along the maturity curve in its use of intelligent automation, including applications of AI. A new wave of solutions demands an architecture that can enable implementation at scale with great ease and speed of deployment. It has to be technology-agnostic and have high flexibility to take advantage of innovations constantly bubbling up in a dynamic AI ecosystem. And it has to enable high degrees of customization based on business needs— including flexibility in the choice of AI technologies used in project management.

The modular quality of a microservices-based automation architecture (or microautomation architecture) can do all of this. It supports continuous delivery, independent scaling, and free choice of technology. It overcomes old fragilities and replaces them with a new robustness.

Development and deployment teams can work more productively in a "fail fast and learn" mode, knowing that because they are working independently, failures can be spotted quickly and their damage contained; any failure is insulated within a single microautomation. A microautomation framework therefore makes automation both distributed and massively scalable.

When we talk about scale, especially as amplified by the scope of a partner ecosystem, it is just as important for a company taking a clean-slate approach to automation architecture to stress interoperability—enabling automation for very distinct purposes and procured from different partners to freely exchange information. Ensuring this means taking a uniform approach to data, security, and governance.

Weave the Data Fabric

Anyone would say that decision-making is best done with data, but is it possible for it to be *led* by data? What would it mean to let data drive the business?

Consider the software produced by Kensho, which is helping some of the largest trading desks in the world crawl through reams of data and market-moving information, searching for correlations between world events and their impacts on asset prices. Analysts using its data-driven investigative analysis tools and machine learning algorithms are able to discover, visualize, and understand complex relationships hidden in massive amounts of data. And that leads them to investment theories that are more rigorous and defensible.[1]

It is possible, then, to be led by data—at least at the individual decision level—but it's safe to say it must be highly trusted data. Data is at the core of data-driven automation (recall it as the first step in the automation ladder, as discussed in Chapter 1) and is the foundation for AI-driven automation. For automation to remain relevant for businesses and to remain a trustworthy basis for decisions, companies need to architect a data fabric to manage and govern huge volumes of data.

What does the term *data fabric* refer to? Think of it as a kind of framework or platform. *Fabric* implies that there are many threads that weave together to create a larger entity. The architecture of the fabric is the plan or model of how those different parts all work together and constitute a continuous layer. This is essential if a company hopes to manage all the data gathered, stored, and used by its various functions and units. It allows a framework to be established to judge data as trustworthy and provides the focal point for governance of what would otherwise be a sprawling and chaotic universe of data.

With the growing demand by businesses to put faster data access and better analytics at their managers' fingertips has come the rise of enterprise data fabric: repositories designed to hold vast amounts of raw data in native formats until it is needed by the business. With enterprise data fabric in place, companies have started to gain various benefits. They have been able to centralize enterprise content silos. They are transforming their insight discovery and analytics processes. And they are able to enrich data in ways that are not possible in the source systems.

The key is having effective applications for searching, analyzing, and deriving insights from the massive structured and unstructured data in the enterprise. Increasingly, these are commercially available—in fact, the data fabric market is a dynamic investment space right now. However, even to use vendors' most basic tools requires a degree of sophistication in data architecture.

Put AI at the Core

As the power of AI is increasingly applied to enterprise automation, systems architects are recognizing that it deserves to be more than an afterthought—not just another set of applications to be supported by a long-established foundation. To the contrary, leading-edge users of AI are rethinking their architectures to put AI at their core. By centering whole architectures on machine-learning and deep-learning (neural network) technologies, they greatly expand their capacity to deliver solutions with breakthrough economics—and to gain impressive competitive advantages.

This is one version of a more general principle: if a company wants to harness the full potential of AI, it should make it the core of its automation strategy. It should be "AI first" in its thinking about strategy and architecture. If that phrase sounds familiar, recall how businesses took off after the advent of the web and began capitalizing on the opportunity to reengineer their processes to take more full advantage of the new possibilities of electronic commerce. The mantra was to transform a company's business model to make it "digital first" in its operations.

By analogy, we're now entering the era of intelligent automation, and in the same way, it's time to proceed in an AI-first way. Automation teams are building and managing solutions that are AI-driven from the ground up, rather than trying to layer AI's intelligence on top of systems whose designers never anticipated AI. They're starting with clean-slate visions of disruptive innovation and new market creation, and sketching out how AI solutions and platforms could make them real. AI for business is taking human-and-machine collaboration to the next level. Expect more organizations to reengineer the experiences that bring technology and people together to solve problems and get work done. Paradoxically, the most human-centric of those solutions will turn out to have AI at their core.

Human-Centric Automation

Thanks to advances in natural language processing, computer vision, voice recognition, and machine learning, technology interfaces are becoming invisible. Finally, machines can adapt to how humans prefer to work, rather than the other way around.

Elegant and simple experiences are the new normal. With systems that can talk, listen, see, and understand, companies can now reimagine systems to empower new human-machine relationships with natural conversation, simple touches, and abundant personalization.

Human-centric automation is already upending decades of conventional thinking about human-machine interaction, along with many adjacent processes. Just consider that the main interface we use today—the keyboard—has been around since commercial typewriters were first introduced in 1874. Now, interfaces can start putting humans at the center of everything, leveraging their natural talents and serving their true needs.

Human-Centric Development

Human-centric design will become the key to unlock better customer experiences and better employee engagement, too. On both sides, it focuses on understanding the needs of the people using the system. Some of this empathic development will proceed from design thinking methods and from design teams that represent more diverse perspectives and disciplines.[2]

Capital One, for example, uses customer-centric design to compete in what many see as a thoroughly commoditized market for consumer credit by focusing on differentiated user experiences. The company took time to speak directly with customers and overcome the preconceived beliefs of some of its analysts. New user-centric processes are helping the company define and solve the most important customer pain points in a way that is data-driven, repeatable, and agile.[3]

Increasingly, however, the human focus will be deepened by data, as feedback is gathered and analyzed continuously and automatically from people going about their daily tasks, using connected technologies to accomplish objectives.

Human-Centric Tools

No company should wait to experiment with the more user-friendly forms of technology emerging around it. Its managers might see applications of AI, extended reality, and voice recognition happening in consumer products right now—and some of the applications might feel gimmicky. But these technologies are evolving exponentially and will burst onto the enterprise scene over the next few years. As reported in thejournal.com, IDC predicts augmented and virtual reality headsets are set to show a compound annual growth rate of 41 percent through 2025.[4]

Early experimentation and hands-on experience are the best ways to start socializing and imagining the commercial possibilities of these technologies as they mature. Drishti, for instance, is a solution designed with the National Association for the Blind in India, which provides help for the visually impaired through smartphones. Using AI technologies such as image recognition, natural language processing, and natural language generation, the solution narrates to the user the number of people in a room, their ages and genders, and even their emotions based on facial expressions. It can also be used to describe text from books, documents, and currency notes, as well as to identify physical obstructions like glass doors.[5]

Human-centric technologies like this may occur to a company's marketers first as enhancements to the offerings the company sells to customers. They can just as easily find their way into the operations of the business itself, combining powerful technology and human-centric design to create tomorrow's advantage.

Move to the Cloud

For some, applications in the cloud may seem like yesterday's news. But for many, there is still much to do to truly exploit the transformative potential of cloud services. That's because the cloud isn't the finish line—it's the starting point, with edge computing right behind.

Cloud computing is essential because it enables companies to use other technologies, including AI and analytics. As such, the cloud serves as a catalyst for innovation. Consider how Salesforce is benefiting from its own cloud-based AI technology, Einstein, to improve business performance. Salesforce's original breakthrough innovation was its customer relationship management software, which salespeople and their managers around the globe use constantly via the cloud to do sales forecasting, pipeline management, and sales organization management. Einstein, launched in 2016, now sits above these and other functions as a smart layer that has access to all the data they contain, whether it came from email, calendars, social media, or formal activity-tracking entries. This is the treasure trove of data that its predictive models learn from to provide new insights to sales professionals on what has worked well (or not worked) in the past.[6]

Or take a lesson from Alibaba Group's financial arm, Ant Group (formerly Ant Financial), which uses cloud services and AI solutions to offer a range of services in mobile payments, banking, insurance, and wealth management.[7] Cloud services and AI are embedded across multiple processes and product lines—adapting to each as needed. As a result, the company can instantly assess the credit risks of underserved people who may not have bank accounts and even target them with loan offers. It can also enable customers to snap photos after an automobile accident to file claims with their insurers in just a few seconds. Ant has transferred innovations and lessons at scale across the organization. And it's gone even further, offering its AI capabilities to external ecosystem partners.[8] For example, Caifu Hao, an

AI-powered corporate account on the Ant platform, has brought tangible benefits to 27 fund management companies.[9] On average, this has allowed these companies to reduce overall costs by 50 percent, increase daily visitors tenfold, and attract a threefold increase in investments by returning customers.

Business is benefiting instantly from a wide variety of cloud services, with providers offering on-demand access to servers, storage, databases, networking, software, analytics, and intelligence. When an automation team takes a cloud-native approach, it means that cloud approaches are embedded in the solutions through every phase from DevOps to deployment, and in all the toolkits employed. Among other benefits, this means that changes can be deployed in mere minutes, even seconds, because the need for them has been well anticipated.

With so many services moving to the cloud, automation applications and the automation platforms will also have to migrate there eventually, so a company's cloud migration strategy should encompass its automation platforms and applications as well. This is no small challenge for an organization full of people trained and experienced with monolithic applications and architectures.

Any team that has moved from monolithic applications to building features and functions in the cloud has discovered how different the process can be. Suddenly, they need to focus on issues that weren't issues before, such as communication with other components. They quickly learn the perils of not standardizing APIs at the outset, and the extra layer of maintaining the components that are lightweight and stateless. It's worth it, they know, because taking advantage of the cloud allows a business to scale a solution in an agile and cost-effective way. It makes their software standardized, scalable, and fast to deploy. But the learning curve can be hard, nonetheless.

The increasing adoption of cloud computing services and the emergence of AI and machine-learning technologies are allowing companies to use intelligent automation to make decisions on known problems, predict issues, and provide diagnostic information to reduce the operational overhead for engineers. For a large-scale automation effort, working in a business cloud-computing environment makes organizations more efficient, strategic, and insight-driven. Cloud computing offers businesses more flexibility, agility, and cost savings by hosting data and applications in the cloud.

Architect for Security

In an era of unrelenting cyberattacks and all too frequent intrusions, it is essential to lay the right foundations for current and future security. Every organization that handles private, sensitive, or proprietary data must have strong protocols for how data is created, processed, shared, stored, and destroyed. Considerations of time must factor into data management. Clearly, for example, financial data is more sensitive before the close of a quarter or year than after a close. There should be clear and effective policies, processes, and systems to protect organizational data from exposure, with the risk tolerance of the organization established by prevailing laws, regulations, and predictions of customer impact. The rules for compliance will vary according to the risk tolerance of the company regarding specific types of data and possibilities for exposure.

Consider how the Republic of Estonia has streamlined citizen experiences by enabling fast, secure data sharing between 52,000 government organizations and private enterprises. All public data, from medical records to residency information, is exclusively stored by local offices. But when completing a task that requires cross-departmental information—creating a birth certificate or filing a police report, for instance—government employees can quickly execute the transaction by automatically authenticating identity or verifying access to deliver a seamless user experience.[10]

In a global organization, this security system should be subject to a formal governance framework, managed by a dedicated, multidisciplinary team. This team needs to ensure comprehensive coverage of the automated and AI applications deployed throughout the enterprise to protect the data models from poisoning partners and customers of the business—which are often global and quite diverse.

For example, many banks operate globally through partners, sometimes thousands of them, who process cards, mortgages and loans, and insurance claims. Likewise, a global pharmaceutical company might have contractual connections to hundreds of university researchers and partner labs, thousands of doctors working with clinical trials, several manufacturing partners, and multiple shipping companies responsible for distribution. Altogether, these commercial relationships make up a large ecosystem, many parts of which are handling sensitive information about customers and intellectual property. Securing and keeping this data private is a complex challenge.

Now add regulations to that complex ecosystem. Few companies in the twenty-first century operate in industries that are not subject to complicated government rules, such as the payment card industry (PCI) regulations on sellers that accept credit card payments; the North American Electric Reliability Corporation Critical Infrastructure Protection (NERC CIP) rules for North American utilities; the CBEST laws governing banking in the United Kingdom; the contents of CFR 21 Part 11 for pharmaceutical companies; the Health Information Trust Alliance (HITRUST) regulations for all organizations involved in US healthcare; the rules imposed by the US National Institute of Standards and Technology (NIST); the quality standards imposed by ISO 27001; or any one of numerous others.

In fact, just within the domain of cybersecurity and data privacy, companies must prove their compliance with more than 300 regulations. All these regulations call for a management system made up of many elements that collectively safeguard information of many kinds. Each company needs to establish client data protection validations, audits, and governance models that offer confidence that it can prevent, detect, and recover from security breaches. To the extent that an intelligent automation solution interacts with separate systems and relies on heavy volumes of data, it must have the benefit of an architecture with the security controls to manage the cyber risks. Governance should give transparency to all relevant stakeholders and have a security alerts management system.

Security is fundamental to customers' confidence and trust, and where it is reasonably assured, adoption of automation solutions goes far more smoothly. If the customer becomes skeptical or trust is lost, automation adoption slows down and an initiative may ultimately fail. At the same time, just as security supports automation success, automation can support security.

In many companies, automation of security updates is already greatly reducing the costs of maintenance and operations. Likewise, security software can detect missing patches in hybrid cloud environments and automatically take the necessary steps to deploy the correct patches and configuration changes to close these exposures. Finally, to ensure effective alignment with today's hybrid realities, teams need solutions that offer cloud-based implementation, while enabling automated management of on-premises data centers and multiclouds.

Make It Platform-Centric

Companies today are increasingly evolving their business models by adopting platform strategies, essentially shifting the locus of their value creation from selling individually popular products to providing layers of infrastructure that allow many more products to be developed and delivered, whether by the company itself or by others. To understand the strategy, think of Microsoft, whose Windows platform has so dominated the desktop market. Its platform-centric approach has allowed it to expand its footprint in customers' operations by steadily adding well-integrated solutions and thereby gaining a competitive edge over its rivals. Another outstanding example of a platform strategy is Amazon's. Early on, it realized that the way to build the most powerful and efficient operational environment to serve its own consumer and enterprise customers would be to scale up those information-processing and logistical strengths and make them available to other sellers.

Along the same lines, pursuing a platform-centric approach in the context of automation is about building a robust foundation of technologies, standards, frameworks, and workflows, and making it available to support automation projects across an entire business. As a result, innovation on a platform occurs much faster as compared to a siloed automation approach or even an automation product-based approach. One continuous landscape is established for all in-house systems, partner systems, and individual business unit automation applications. This approach enables a company to achieve a kind of hybrid automation operating model—imposing standards and practices on a centralized basis while still allowing individual business units and project teams to follow the automation approaches that they determine make most sense for them.

The point of a platform is to create a one-stop shop for all those teams in an organization wanting to explore the possibilities for intelligent automation. It provides capabilities across the whole spectrum of automation, ranging from planning automation, tracking, and monitoring the value realization from automation; predicting issues impacting business; identifying complex dependencies across the systems interacting with the automation; and in harvesting the automation assets across the enterprise. The platforms also feature their own applications of analytics and AI to help guide their users in assembling optimal solutions.

For our business executives, who traditionally would have spent many days on discovery and integration of multiple proprietary and third-party tools, all this is very welcome leverage. Delivering to their clients is a lot simpler with automation and integration functionality such as plug-and-play modularity, single-click provisioning, virtual agents, and mobile alerts.

Having a robust platform pays off in speed, agility, productivity, and quality. It can be used to centralize automation practices and solutions. It will make the users as well as the automation engineers more efficient and skilled, thereby allowing them to focus on higher-value work. Meanwhile, the company can have the holistic management benefit of knowing that people are drawing on the same selected group of assets and that they represent the best of the ecosystem.

Reimagine Business Models

When boundaries disappear, new spaces open up. This creates a new landscape—one where new ideas and unconventional partnerships can flourish.

Making a company's automation ecosystem more integrated and centralized can reveal opportunities not only to scale specific innovations but also to make change at the level of its business model. It can open up possibilities to partner with other enterprises in solving significant business, consumer, and societal problems. It can make it easier to piggyback on technology advances to reduce the friction in today's processes, transactions, and business models. And it can allow innovative ideas to be implemented and scaled with new speed and agility.

Sound Familiar?

It may seem that only well-established companies in industrial manufacturing sectors would be struggling to create the kind of new, agile automation systems capability we've been describing here. The truth is that a quarter century into the internet era, even digital native companies are typically saddled with monolithic enterprise architectures.

Another example is a company that just over a decade ago was one of the biggest disruptors of the travel industry. When it first launched its business, speed to market was paramount, so getting the right long-term, scalable architecture in place wasn't a priority. Then the company faced the challenge of scaling its platform to meet the demands of a growing customer base and geographic expansion. As part of a decoupling initiative, it migrated its platform to microservices, which allowed the company to rapidly respond to change and add new features as it experiences explosive growth.

Many other companies face the same need to update. The leaders among them will opt for flexible, uniform, and scalable architectures. They will accept the hard work that will go into redesigning solutions for these new environments, along with the implications for talent reskilling and mindset shifts. They know the benefits will outweigh these costs as they gain the ability to respond more quickly to market demands, like seamless customer payments. The laggards, unfortunately, will shy away from the difficulties of moving away from rigid IT architectures, never quite seeing the shift as urgent, and only adding over time to the unwieldy and unworkable architectures they have in place. We know which route allows a company to gain the greater edge from its investments in innovation. By embracing the six principles described here, an organization can take that route.

Platform-Centric Approach for Improving the Speed to Innovate

A large multinational energy company designed its future vision with automation at the core. The company took a platform-centric approach to accelerate the innovations to market. With open and plug-and-play architecture, the company could quickly adapt to the technology changes in a nonintrusive manner. It made its technology and automation solutions future-proof and very agile and quick to respond to market dynamics. This has helped the company accelerate innovation and ensure that automation is scalable and flexible for future-ready systems. The company leverages design thinking and rapid prototyping as its continuous innovation approach and is ensuring a sustainable automation journey.

Key Takeaways

▸ Most companies do not have technology infrastructures capable of supporting high levels of intelligent automation. Legacy systems in place typically fall short in six ways.

▸ Leading enterprise adopters of intelligent automation are migrating quickly to infrastructures that are designed to be adaptive, to interact with rich data fabrics, and to have AI at their core. The right architectures for intelligent automation are also cloud-based, security-filled, and platform-centric.

▸ Building a modern IT architecture is a big challenge, but far more complicated when the need is to migrate from an old architecture that is fast becoming obsolete. High-visibility projects can help drive high-priority upgrades.

7

Inspire the Transformation

As many think tanks and other researchers look into how automation can be expected to impact workers, a study from the Brookings Institution gave some cause for alarm: it claimed that as many as a quarter of the jobs Americans hold today might in the near future be handed over to machines. Low-skilled workers will be hardest hit, one of its authors told a reporter: "If your job is boring and repetitive, you're probably at great risk of automation." But, he cautioned, even well-educated knowledge workers who spend only some portion of their day on routine work will be affected: "Virtually all jobs are going to begin to experience some pressure from automation."[1]

In some ways, the fear of the unknown effects on jobs and careers is the biggest obstacle to progress in intelligent automation. People in workplaces can see it as a slippery slope: start handing tasks to machines and before you know it, there won't be enough work for people to do. Most CEOs we know, however, do not envision headcount reductions in their organizations; most, in fact, plan to *grow* their workforces, as their people, better leveraged by automation, are able to produce dramatically more value for customers. The key to keeping workforce anxiety from allowing everyone to benefit from automation is to reduce the uncertainty.

Chapter 5 made the case that for any organization hoping to introduce intelligent automation at scale, an operating model is essential. There is another big consideration, too, however, as an automation team goes about planning the plan. This is the realm of people and the need for a *talent model*.

Success will depend on having the right team structures and the right competencies with the appropriate mix of talents and skills for the solutions envisioned. How this is accomplished will vary depending on the maturity of the organization with regard to intelligent automation. For example, automation projects wouldn't be led by only IT people, although the team should include technically talented people from the beginning. If skills are lacking to provide the needed industry knowledge, there might be training or other forms of enablement that could be provided. These are among the matters addressed in this chapter.

The benefit of a clearly laid out talent model, however, is not just to get the right skills in place—it's also to get people's heads in the right place. Mindset is a big contributor to the success or failure of intelligent automation efforts, and it is shaped by people's expectations of how they may be affected by a change. If a positive, people-focused plan is broadly communicated, the fear of the unknown can dissipate. Few people, if they are assured that they still have a future in an organization, are disappointed at the thought that they might do less boring and repetitive work. To the contrary, they can begin to be forces for change themselves, identifying ways to enhance their jobs and get more done with less effort. Make the talent plan clear, and it can help inspire the transformation.

The Good and Bad News About the Workforce

Here's the bad news: people are hard, expensive, and time-consuming to change, whether we're talking about their skill sets or their sentiments. Recall that our discussion of barriers to automation (in Chapter 2) started with people issues: the talent shortages that get cited in survey after survey and the perennial change management challenges as the nature of jobs changes. In a 2018 joint World Economic Forum/Accenture research study, nearly half of the executives surveyed said that traditional job descriptions are obsolete as machines take on routine tasks and as people move to project-based work. Twenty-nine percent of leaders report that they've extensively redesigned jobs.[2]

But here's the good news: exactly because it is hard to simply upgrade people in the way that companies can update software, people will remain the best bet for gaining and sustaining competitive advantage. It has always been true that human competencies are the real edge in a competitive business, and somewhat paradoxically this will become even more true in an era of heightened automation. Machine capabilities are wondrous when introduced, but consider how quickly they spread across companies, sectors, and economies to become table stakes to compete. Meanwhile, the more that mundane tasks get automated, the more impactful the higher-order tasks become—and they are precisely the tasks that remain in human hands.

Brent Kedzierski is head of Learning Strategy and Innovation at Royal Dutch Shell, a company in the intelligent automation vanguard. As Kedzierski sees it, the point of these new tools is to make people capable of greater things, not to have them do less. "Think about the sensor or drone that can continuously acquire data that was once only possible with a worker going up in a crane," he says. "Think about the worker that has the benefit of curated insights to support higher-order decision-making or problem-solving. Think about the possibilities of tracking performance, comparing outcome trends, and then using intelligent analytics to identify new opportunities."[3] Kedzierski believes intelligent automation is creating a whole new world of possibilities and even "redefining how our industry operates," but he also stresses that this means "the competencies of our workforce will need to evolve." He expects people to contribute more in ways that computers cannot:

> Automation will drive the need to raise the cognitive and interpersonal abilities of our workforce. Automation will enhance basic decision-making and problem-solving, opening the door for workers to interact with more data at higher intellectual levels. The wealth of insights created by big data will also enable colleagues to collaborate in more thoughtful ways that require greater interpersonal skills and sensemaking.

This is a company that recognizes that human talent is ultimately what will give it the edge over competitors—but that gaining that edge demands that people's creativity and judgment be leveraged by systems capable of sophisticated information processing.

Reskilling Technology Talent

The immediate talent challenges most companies perceive as they begin their intelligent automation journeys are in the ranks of their business operations, systems development, and deployment groups. Most of these professionals were trained and gained their years of experience on older generations of software and hardware. But successful automation deployments and scaling up require people with deep understanding of business processes, robotic process automation, and AI technologies.

In survey after survey, employers report severe talent shortages. And with significant upshifts expected in skill requirements, the gaps are likely to increase—dramatically. By one estimate, for workers seeking to remain in their current roles, the share of core skills that will change by 2025 is 40 percent, and 50 percent of all employees will need reskilling.[4] The talent of the future will need to bring creative problem-solving to the enterprise, in addition to strong digital, operational, and domain expertise.

Research by our colleagues at Accenture suggests that the workforce of the future is moving rapidly toward three types:

- **Machine workforce (robots/platform/AI solutions):** This will become the primary way to execute everything that can be automated.
- **Transaction human workforce:** While enterprises are automating all that can be automated, there will be a need for human interventions to process transactions that cannot be automated.
- **Expert workforce:** As simple items are being largely automated, humans will be needed to work in increasingly complex areas. They will make more exception-related decisions and will be large contributors

to ideas on how and where to automate and what information can help them in making better decisions.

It is also becoming clear that the emerging expert workforce consists of people falling into two major camps: the expert workforce that is adopting automation solutions within IT, and the expert workforce that is driving the creation of value for customers in the business. As for the first group, they are the ones enabling intelligent automation, and include such experts as tech masters (including automation developers and architects), data scientists, AI champions, process architects, and business advisors (who embrace and are the ambassadors of automation within the delivery organization).

The latter group, the experts driving customer value, are being significantly helped by automation. In particular, they excel thanks to new levels of access to data from predictive models, and by spending more of their time focusing on high-impact business decisions, as opposed to having time eaten up by efforts to extract and process information. In a pharmaceutical company we know, for example, highly qualified medical professionals involved in what is known as the covigilance process had been spending many hours reading medical reports. Now, assisted by AI advisors, these valuable knowledge workers are able to devote more of their attention to the higher-order tasks of considering the implications of the information extracted and making better decisions as a result.

As organizations struggle to find the right resources to implement intelligent automation effectively, they have two basic options: they can hire new people with more relevant competencies or invest in skills training to cultivate these new talents in the current staff. Most will have to do both. In either case, building automation and AI talent will also require cultivating a stronger culture of automation within the IT organization.

Culture is a term that gets thrown around quite a bit in management writing, but often in a vague way. Essentially, it is the distinctive collection of shared values, recognized symbols, habitual behaviors, and prevailing assumptions that defines how an organization goes about solving problems and meeting objectives. Culture is more deeply rooted in people's psychology than in tangible tools and standard operating procedures. A common way of referring to culture is to talk about "the way we do things around here."[5] Whole organizations have their cultures, but within them, every function, department, and enduring group has its own culture. The IT organization is no exception. Any transformation of "how it does things" must go beyond investing in a new toolkit and putting people through skills training. It must shift their attitudes and beliefs about what is important to accomplish.

Putting in place a microservices architecture, for example, does not only call upon new tools. It involves mindset shifts and cultural change. It implies a greater separation between infrastructure and application teams than IT organizations have been accustomed to having. This change has to be deftly managed.

As another example, many observers have noted the emergence of a new kind of developer: they produce code without custom scripting. This a good reminder that the technology talent portfolio is always in flux. Whenever a new technological approach arises, there is an infusion of a different type of talent that has to be well managed.

A Model for Automation Talent Development
At Accenture, it was obvious that succeeding in the era of intelligent automation would mean serious, sustained training of our

experienced workforce. Yes, we continue to recruit new talent constantly and identify people familiar with the technologies defining the landscape today, like AI, automation, industry domain, Agile, DevOps, digital security, and deep learning.

But at the same time, it was never an option to walk away from legions of talented technologists who were just as eager as the company is to keep their skills current. To home-grow the workforce we needed, we built an automation and AI career model. At the core of it is a curriculum that everyone in the organization goes through, graduating to new levels as they master sets of skills. Without implying that every kind of organization should do the same, it's worth walking through its steps to note the skills and competencies it seeks to build.

The easy way to present this career model is with a pyramid structure, which captures the fact that as one progresses through it, one moves up to higher-level skills that build on previously obtained ones and also finds oneself in more select company. (See Figure 7.1.) As people start building their automation competencies, they enter the first tier of the pyramid and are referred to as automation primes. We need many such contributors, because they do the bulk of the actual scripting of the myriad automation solutions we deliver to our clients. Automation primes are delivery team members who can conceptualize and implement automation solutions within a client engagement to establish highly productive delivery systems.

The next two levels feature two career-path possibilities: automation architects and senior automation architects. They are trained to architect, plan, execute, and provide appropriate governance for a successful automation project. They have to have executed at least one successful initiative and reached the point of measuring its delivered benefits before we certify them at this level.

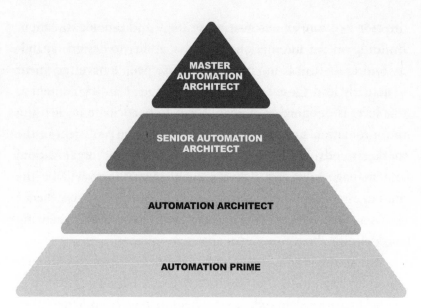

FIGURE 7.1 **Automation Specialization Program**

The automation architect is focused on devising the automation solution. This translates to different learning objectives for the two. Training for automation architects gives them the technology expertise to assess the business application and IT landscape, to identify automation and optimization opportunities, to define the automation plan and the client road map, to create automation solutions and quantify automation savings and benefits to the client, to design automation assets, and to lead complex implementation at scope. In sum, automation architects learn the skills to build automation across every aspect of software, from development and testing to maintenance and infrastructure. They need to be able to define the whole automation solution and lay out a practical automation blueprint for building it.

The highest level in our career model consists of master automation architects, who work along with a client's automation director to create an automation strategy and provide direction. Building on the automation architects' ability to design capability and cross-functional programs, these people have the talent to actually lead those ambitious efforts. Our training content at this level is designed to prepare them to participate in devising the automation strategy of the organization; be proficient in the market trends and design the road map for the organization; and manage sales and delivery enablement. They will be the ones to establish policies and practices for automation excellence across all engagements within their portfolio by conceptualizing and defining cross-functional automation ideas.

The automation talent model is aligned to drive the automation maturity model that we discussed in Chapter 1. Every step of the maturity demands a set of competencies to achieve the maturity at that level. Figure 7.2 depicts a representative set of competencies for each step.

Throughout this journey, the curriculum is designed not only to train people on the relevant automation tools, technologies, and skills, but also to establish a broad culture of readiness and enthusiasm for human-machine collaboration. To be certified as an automation prime, it is not enough to have learned scripting tools and be able to identify the specific robotic cross-actions that make up script-based solutions. Primes also learn to demonstrate measurable outcomes—helping drive home that this is important progress to keep building on. An automation architect shouldn't only be a coding expert but should also embrace Agile and design thinking to map out the right automation journey. Each level needs to mark a measurable advance in terms of gaining technical expertise and contributing to the culture.

Again, the point of this section is not to offer a precise prescription to other organizations but rather to raise some key questions: Should we have our own framework for internal talent

INTELLIGENT
- Enterprise Automation Strategy
- Enterprise Automation Architecture
- AI Technologies Expertise
- Microservices Architecture

AI Driven

PREDICTIVE
- Data & Process Diagnostics
- Data, Integration, Analytics
- Integration Architecture

Data Driven

EFFICIENT
- Robotic Process Automation Scripting
- Enterprise Architecture Fundamentals

RPA Driven

OPTIMIZE
- Business Process Diagnostics
- Technology Diagnostics
- Cloud Architecture
- IT Architecture

Process Driven

FOUNDATION
- Automation Scripting (using R, Python, ABAP, Shell Scripting, Perl, etc.)
- Methods and Tools

Tools Driven

| Automation Prime | Automation Architect | Sr. Automation Architect | Master Automation Architect |

FIGURE 7.2 Automation Talent Model

development and tracking? What should it look like? What skills would it build and what roles would it prepare people for? Finally, how might it go beyond building technical expertise and also be a force for positive evolution in our IT group's culture, boosting its readiness and enthusiasm to embrace automation at scale?

Given today's limited pool of talent on the market, increasing numbers of organizations will be asking these questions. Many will find that the only way to get the intelligent automation skills they need in sufficient numbers of people is to focus on internal training. To be sure, this training content doesn't all have to be internally developed. Enterprise-grade, road-tested digital learning platforms already exist to reskill workforces at scale. It would be irresponsible not to leverage whatever material has already been well developed by top vendors.

Today, a large part of Accenture's workforce is focused on applying automation to help our clients compete effectively. The automation talent model has brought and continues to bring thousands of professionals to a higher level of automation competency. This is a good example of how humans and machines can collaborate to bring greater value than if either worked alone. The future is all about the human + machine mode, infused with data and insights that will fuel growth. Having a career framework in our organization, where people are encouraged to scale a pyramid of automation expertise, has enabled the higher level of automation competency.

At Accenture, this talent model has been successful, and we can share a few secrets to that success. First, it features transparency. The workers on the receiving end of this talent model had complete transparency into how we personalized it to suit each of their career journeys through mechanisms like Job Buddy. This is Accenture's patented AI advisor, which can be consulted for advice on how to reskill and upskill oneself based on input offered on past experience and roles. Transparency is also driven through clear communication of the impact to everyone's career.

Second, our talent model is designed to inspire learning. Becoming a successful automation or AI engineer requires structured, focused, and continuous learning. Among the creative ways that Accenture builds its learning culture are by tailoring highly personalized learning paths, providing immersive learning experiences, and supporting microlearning—in other words, we provide focused content that can be mastered in a short time, allowing for great flexibility. We also believe in "learning through teaching," having seen the impact on our learning culture of asking people in the process of reskilling to immediately turn around and explain it to others.

Reskilling AI's New Users

To deliver real impact, automation solutions can't have well-prepared minds only on the production side of the project; they also need them on the consumption side. Managers should ask: Are the business users impacted prepared to adopt this? What kind of user trainings and instructions should be given? Are the people whose work processes will be affected prepared to work effectively with the new technologies? What kind of training or support could help them?

The business users using the application have to adopt new ways of interactions with the applications or usage or process flow. The workers in the various groups who will use the new solutions will have to learn different work steps and adopt new ways of working that redefine the relationships among them. Even more substantially, to the extent that automation now relieves them of some time-consuming tasks, it will also help in making informed decisions. Unless the business is equipped to adapt to this change, the automation solution cannot deliver its projected benefits.

In a recent study of companies that had implemented robotic process automation, researchers surveyed the employees whose work was actually affected by the introduction of these tools. The good news was that close to half replied that, "Yes, it has removed some mundane tasks and enabled employees to focus better on their work/customers." Still, that left about the same number reporting that either the investment in robotic process automation had not actually eliminated mundane work, or that it hadn't "enabled employees to focus better on their work/customers." This speaks to a failure not on the technology side but on the matter of how employees are prepared and empowered to turn their attention to other, less mundane tasks.[6]

In a very real sense, users of AI and automation are not just IT pros or technical experts. The end users in the business are often not savvy at all about the underlying technology. The same care should be taken to heighten their experience as is taken in customer relationships. Here are some basic principles for helping not just a tech team, but a whole company embrace automation.

Educate Broadly on the Benefits of Intelligent Automation

First, harking back to the worries outlined at the start of this chapter, it shouldn't be assumed that the automation solutions team will be welcomed with open arms, no questions asked. To the contrary, it might be more realistic to expect a strong undercurrent of suspicion.

It has not been very long since chatbots and conversational agents were first introduced to increase sales. In the early days of chatbots, they didn't yield results as expected. From a management standpoint, they were viewed as highly useful automation, but customers were surprisingly slow to gravitate to the chatbots channel. Multiple factors explain the hesitation, but mostly it came down to how the end user perceived the use of technology. Users often carry forward perceptions they gained from using similar interfaces in other settings. Typically, end users very much value human interaction. The same applies for interactive voice response: even after going through all the automated steps, people often opt to connect to a person. The challenges are educating the users about how to use the technology and creating greater awareness of the value it creates for them.

Workers in other settings may well have the same kinds of misgivings about automation being introduced. It is critical to ensure in advance that the people expected to use a new toolkit don't feel threatened by it. Managers need to build support for a rollout of new technology by helping everyone in the organization—from the top down—understand how it will enhance job quality. The mantra in marketing products has always been to stress benefits, not features, and the same applies here.

Most miners, for example, will likely not object when the result of bringing smart, sensor-equipped machines into the mine means that the risk of undetected toxic leaks is reduced. And when Shell introduced RealWear head-mounted displays for its remote maintenance workers, they weren't a hard sell. Managers didn't spend much time touting the high-tech wizardry behind these head-mounted computers—however fascinating this might be to the software engineers. They emphasized the situations in which, say, a remote worker would find it very useful to use a voice-controlled device to send an image of exactly what he was seeing and get real-time assistance in solving a problem.[7]

The truth is that people thinking about their own workplaces and job structures can usually see quite readily how intelligent automation presents real progress and has positive implications for the future of work. Many of the tasks being automated involve mundane, high-volume, or repetitive processes. By having automation take on those tasks, people get more time to perform the higher-order, nonroutinized jobs that require creative problem solving, innovation, discretionary decision-making, critical analysis, and interpersonal communication.

To get the benefits of automation without alienating talent, our advice is to begin with the workers themselves and something as simple as a sticky-note exercise. We have done this with many teams at the outset of opportunity finding. Everyone writes down all the tasks they routinely perform as part of their jobs, one task per sticky note. Then they add to each note an emoji face—smiling, frowning, or in between—to show how much they value doing that part of their job. Do they learn anything from continuing to do it? Does it give them joy? Clumping the frowns together gives a clear indication of how much of their job they would not mind seeing a machine take off their hands—especially if that meant filling that time with more of the tasks they enjoy.

Consider the New York–based BNY Mellon, which deployed more than 200 bots across its business to drive efficiency and cut out costly errors. This cadre of robotic assistants is accelerating the bank's critical payment processing by reducing the time spent by employees identifying and dealing with data mistakes. Organizational change has been a key part of this innovation. Many of the bank's bots originate from its new global innovation centers, where teams are organized around solving particular problems—with the freedom to reimagine "the art of the possible."[8]

The lesson to other companies is simple: Don't expect to just introduce an automation solution, do some quick how-to training, and leave people to make their peace with it. Plan by thinking: Who are the consumers? How do we get them ready? How will they use this on the ground, and what kind of enablers will be created for them? Make it clear to employees and customers how new tools and technologies can make everyday interactions more engaging.

Create a people-first strategy for transitioning the organization, training on new skills, and implementing the changes. As Shell's Kedzierski puts it, "consider the worker as the center of performance." Be very clear that the intent is to augment and up-level people's current work, as opposed to eliminating positions. Identify internal technology champions who can show their teams how the benefits of automation are showing up elsewhere, whether in other companies in the industry or in their daily lives as consumers. Provide solutions that are accessible and relevant, and that add obvious value to individuals, teams, and work.

Translating the Automation Edge to the Human Edge

The work processes of the future, increasingly powered by intelligent automation, will also—somewhat paradoxically—be more deeply human. They will be designed and implemented in ways that serve humans best, whether the focus is on the worker or customer experience of interacting with the enterprise. Both benefited, for example, from a change fashion retailer H&M aimed at personalizing the customer experience—even, ultimately, to the point of offering individualized products. Designers, now leveraged by AI, have the ability to produce work that truly delights their customers. Meanwhile, keeping automation human-centered can also mean committing to keep people gainfully employed.

At Accenture itself, although we have deployed robotic process automation in our business process outsourcing service line to a degree that it represents the labor of 20,000 people—and that number continues to grow—none of our talented staff lost their jobs as a result. Instead, those affected by the shift of tasks to machines saw their roles migrate to more sophisticated and rewarding tasks as the robots freed them to be more creative. The human-centric approach, we believe, is to take the savings generated by automation and invest them in the high-touch differentiators that matter most—to translate the automation edge to a human edge, too.

Avoid the Mysterious Black Box

Even though most users of technology don't feel the need to understand how it works, there is a difference when the technology strays into cognitive territory. To gain the trust and confidence of humans, AI and other decision-oriented tools should have an understandable process and model for arriving at their conclusions. First and foremost, that means being transparent about the logic and process built into an algorithm; the people in the equation, after all, will inevitably be the ones asked to defend it to other stakeholders (like important customers).

Take Drive PX, NVidia's AI-infused self-driving car platform. Even for the company's own engineers, explaining exactly how Drive PX was teaching itself to drive was proving a challenge. So, they developed a way for the machine to explain its driving style visually. By using video of recently driven streetscapes overlaid with the areas prioritized when making driving decisions, Drive PX is opening up the black box of machine learning and taking a step forward for explainability.[9]

In most intelligent automation solutions, opening up that box also means allowing humans to spot when the logic is off and should be revised to produce better results. It's essential, too, that they understand when and how to step in and take back control to avoid an adverse effect on business performance, brand reputation, regulatory compliance, and above all, human beings themselves.

Evolving Culture

Broadening the perspective on people management, a big area for attention is cultivating a whole organizational culture that is conducive to automation. One part of this we have already briefly discussed: establishing trust that the goal is to augment and enhance people's work rather than eliminate their positions. But bringing about cultural change also calls for inspiring people's imaginations about the possibilities for other applications. More than neutralizing fears, it calls for raising positive expectations. Workers are the ones who see an operation's inefficiencies and quality issues up close. What would it take to get everyone in the habit of saying, "This is rule-based and repetitive—why isn't it automated yet?"

Ideas can come from anywhere. Shell reports, for example, that one of its engineers, Shankar Bhat, "has his 10-year-old daughter, Tanisha, to thank for an idea that helped bring a touch of virtual reality (VR) to safety training procedures in a new deep-water oil project." She had heard from her friends about a shopping center in Kuala Lumpur where there was a VR booth. Visitors could put on goggles, sit in a mechanized chair, and be immersed in a thrilling Jurassic Park–style world of rampaging dinosaurs. When she begged her father to take her there, he saw how the same kind of setup might be useful to Shell.[10]

We mentioned earlier the sticky-note exercise that helps people see automation in a more positive light. In fact, the first use of it was with our own software development teams, and the output included actual targets for automation. We gathered up the most disliked tasks cited by people and collectively asked about each of them: "Can we automate this? We really would prefer not to do it—and we have plenty of other work to consume our time—so could it be handled by a machine?"

People are born problem-solvers, but employers rarely provide much encouragement for frontline workers to question standard operating procedures. Offer that bit of encouragement and people will start pointing to ways their work could be taken to a new level. Start by asking: Where do you spend a large portion of time with little or no payoff? Is it in tracking down status updates, handling customer communications, building reports, sending recurring invoices? Leaders should celebrate personal initiative by recognizing and rewarding anyone whose idea or effort led to automation that had a positive impact on the business.

This will become all the more important as nontechnical workers become increasingly capable of using simple-interface technologies to devise their own automation solutions—some of which will prove scalable. Just as consumers are being equipped to build simple, custom apps through voice commands, gestures, and more to their devices, people will also, as employees, soon be able to act as programmers. Vendors of what are referred to as no-code solutions continue to multiply as demand rises.

A decade ago, IT departments were grappling with the challenge of "bring your own device" (BYOD)—the increasing tendency of employees to bring their own portable hardware and software to work, because they were willing to invest in equipping themselves to be more productive. Now, companies can look forward to "bring your own AI" for the same reason. People motivated to raise their game will play active roles in applying automation. While certainly working to contain the risks this entails, company leaders should ensure their talent is not afraid to experiment and present nontraditional ideas— important components of learning and growing.

Another way of expressing this is to say that organizations should cultivate an ownership culture around automation. As a first step, managers should conduct a kind of cultural audit, assessing whether and how organizational or cultural barriers are currently hindering the development and deployment of automation solutions. Then they should reacquaint themselves with all the classic levers of cultural change. Edgar Schein, an expert on organizational culture change and leadership, boils these down to eight activities:

- ▸ Provide a compelling positive vision
- ▸ Provide formal training
- ▸ Make sure learners are involved in the change policy and execution
- ▸ Provide informal training of relevant groups and teams
- ▸ Provide practice fields, coaches, and feedback
- ▸ Provide positive role models
- ▸ Provide support groups in which learning problems can be aired and discussed
- ▸ Provide systems and structures that are consistent with the new way of thinking and working[11]

Building a culture of innovation and customer-centricity will mean, for many companies, overcoming long-established inertia. A culture of design thinking needs to grow organically. Employees must be able to see the bigger picture and learn to see all the moving parts of an organization as independent systems that are interlinked. They need to understand how change in any one system impacts the other systems and eventually impacts the whole.

Especially in situations where a change of direction creates learning anxieties—that is, the clear need to learn new things and some uncertainty about how hard that learning process will be—these are essential activities to help a workforce see the change as possible and worthwhile. Establishing an ownership culture, founded on trust and transparency, can help ensure that new tools and technologies actually increase employee engagement.

Inspiring Leadership

This brings us, finally, to the people whose buy-in and knowledge are most pivotal in an organization's automation journey: top leadership. By fully understanding the opportunities presented by AI, forward-thinking leaders can become trailblazers for intelligent automation across the enterprise and help unlock a wide range of benefits and better outcomes. But if they choose instead to focus on other priorities and delegate this strategic activity, they will undermine its success in many ways.

Often there is at least one person in the C-suite who appreciates the stakes involved here. If you are that person, do what you can to create forums for other top managers to learn about automation as it is being applied elsewhere, exchange ideas, discuss digital trends, and define workforce goals. We have had success with top teams using design thinking techniques and facilitated sessions to arrive at a vision and action plan that managers can embrace and begin to execute.

In general, it is the technology leadership within enterprises that already sees the vast potential of intelligent automation and how it will inevitably pervade every aspect of business. Meanwhile, there may be others who are receptive to the business case, but who have yet to look beyond the potential of automation to simply cut costs. The companies that will grow and dominate their industries will be those that systematically embrace automation across their organizations, using it to drive the changes to their products, services, and even business models as they continue to transform themselves and their industry.

Change at this level simply cannot happen without senior leadership driving it. Fortunately, there are signs that this is happening. In a recent survey of global business leaders, over half (52 percent) expressed a belief that within five years it would become more important for senior executives to understand new and emerging technologies, including AI, than to be well versed in traditional management domains like sales and marketing. This, in fact, was the top quality respondents chose for C-suite executives entering an era of tech-augmented workforces and rapidly evolving technologies.[12]

Prepare to Be Leveraged

Perhaps it should be no surprise that the past several years has seen a deluge of new intelligent automation solutions into American workplaces and, simultaneously, a record-low level of unemployment and record-high participation rate in the nation's economy. The effects of automation do not seem to include a decimation of jobs and the creation of a dehumanized future.

Pioneering companies are instead using intelligent automation to drive new and much more productive relationships between people and machines. This is not simply a triumph of the automation technologies and their developers. It would not be possible except that workers have shifted to a culture of ownership, responding to human-centric development processes, and exhibiting a frontier spirit of experimentation.[13]

At the online personal-styling company Stitch Fix, for example, stylists didn't see AI as a threat when it was introduced. They quickly started calling their machine coworkers their "new BFFs," because the AI helped stylists do their job better and faster by algorithmically winnowing down the overwhelming number of possible clothing and accessory recommendations.[14, 15] They also liked what they saw in the recommendations. After all, the data and AI that underlie intelligent automation are mostly just the digital expression of humans' experience over time. Ultimately, the end game of intelligent automation is customers who have a better experience and employees who are more engaged. It only achieves this if it allows teams to focus on higher-level tasks that are far more fulfilling than the work more easily managed by machines.

Leaders understand that investing in talent and building a cultural affinity for automation is the best way to capitalize on evolving information technology. It is true that these systems will keep progressing, and so must the workforce—within the IT group and throughout the ranks of the organization. In fact, a workforce immersed in yesterday's technologies is one of the biggest obstacles to creating the expansive, flexible, human-centric systems necessary for success. It can seem that intelligent automation is just the ongoing, accelerating transfer of more and more tasks from human to machine. But look again. This is not a vision of a world without people—humans are still central to adaptable systems, collaborating with machines to make reliable decisions and take confident action exponentially faster.

The real power of intelligent automation is its ability to fundamentally change traditional ways of operating, for businesses and individuals. Smart machines offer strengths and capabilities that are different from but highly complementary to people's talents. As they grow in sophistication, they will allow people to do things better—and to do better things.

The Human-Technology Connection

More than one utility company is currently exploring how 3D, extended reality, and AI technologies can help operators train their powerplant personnel in any scenario, at any time. With virtual reality tools, they can design training scenarios and simulations that would otherwise be too inaccessible, expensive, or dangerous if carried out in the real world. This kind of simulation is also useful in emergency-response planning in large, complex sites like shopping malls and theme parks. The humanlike interaction with technology can make a notable impact, not just by training workers but also by making facilities safer for everyone.

Key Takeaways

- No organization can realize the potential of intelligent automation if its people are not capable and enthusiastic supporters of the change.
- New skills will be required, and not only on the technical side. The large and diverse employee user base that needs to embrace the new tools will need training and development, too.
- The culture will need to shift to being a more change-ready and growth-oriented one, in which people are eager to have their human strengths better leveraged by technology.
- Leadership will have to be all-in on AI, signaling enthusiasm with both words and actions and helping others see its potential to make life better for workers, customers, and society.

Sustain the Gains

I t's a common problem in all kinds of change initiatives: a transformation is accomplished with great effort and enthusiasm, and the proof points are documented to show it is working. Success is celebrated, vendors are happily paid, testimonials are gathered, and the glowing case studies are publicized. Everyone dusts off their hands and prepares to dive into the next new thing. They move on.

And then the success stalls. Forward momentum ceases. Backsliding may even begin.

We knew when we set out on this book project that we would have to devote a chapter to the challenge of sustaining the value, because the frequent experience of companies is that backsliding does occur. Even if a company's managers are not terribly ambitious in the automation journey they planned—it might be that they are happy to stay at level two or three in their automation maturity—if they don't actively work to keep whatever automation advantage they have managed to gain, it quickly begins to erode.

This is why we insist on including a last principle in the automation strategies we help map, which we call "sustain." In truth, it would be even better to call it "sustain and strengthen." Simply maintaining the status quo is not a viable option as the technologies involved in intelligent automation continue to advance, and the problems they were applied to solve keep evolving, too. To hold onto an automation advantage, organizations have to keep pushing the envelope, looking for ways to take the innovation forward and staying on pace with overall progress in the market.

This chapter offers advice for sustaining the return on investments in intelligent automation, recognizing that this is a challenge on multiple levels. With regard to individual projects, solutions can atrophy if they aren't maintained; even more so, at the level of the overall enterprise, it is a constant challenge to keep up the momentum of identifying fresh automation opportunities and applying innovative solutions. We stress the importance of fueling forward motion and building agility by constantly tracking industry trends, embracing new developments in technology (e.g., automation in the cloud), and remaining relevant in a world of always-changing market demands. We emphasize the hard but necessary work of building a culture that welcomes productive change and nurtures the talent to constantly innovate. And we underscore, once again, the power of a committed leadership team willing to keep imagining and pursuing better ways for human efforts to be empowered and elevated.

Jump-Start with Energy

This advice may come late in the text of this book, but in the context of an automation initiative, thinking about it should happen early. Initiatives should start with as much of a bang as they can, with strong resource commitments and communications crafted to appeal to hearts and minds. Leaders need to get as many people as possible—from businesspeople to analysts to data scientists—excited about the future state they have in mind. Usually, when forward progress falters, at least part of the problem is that not enough energy was injected into the system at the outset.

This energy level can be tricky to gauge: People often give the appearance of being on board in the early days of a change campaign. They seem to get at least the logic behind the plan and appreciate the urgency of putting capabilities in place, since competitors are undoubtedly spotting the same opportunity. Often, they are genuinely hopeful about the new ways of working and optimistic about the better results they will yield. So managers may get the impression that the people speaking up with enthusiasm and behaving in proactive ways are representative of the whole organization's eagerness for the change. But all that can be deceptive. For every vocal supporter, there may not be 10 coming behind with just as much gusto. There may be just the one.

The anthropologist Margaret Mead famously said: "Never doubt that a small group of thoughtful, committed citizens can change the world; indeed, it's the only thing that ever has." Certainly, all change begins at that level—and a small group can sometimes get surprisingly far on their own talent and determination. But rather than count on that, managers trying to bring about lasting transformations should rally groups as large as they can. As the change management guru John Kotter insists: "Unless you have enough people who want to make something happen, who are driven not only by just the logic of it, but something more emotional—the heart's in it, too—it's just too small an engine, if you will, to carry a big organization across a finish line that's a long way away."[1] This means that the engine of change must be constantly refueled, but even more fundamentally, Kotter notes, it means that right at the beginning, managers must summon the organizational energy that will propel the desired change and give it a strong chance of making it through to the end.

Energy Company Speeds New Capabilities and Reduces Operating Costs

The IT organization of a large multinational energy company offers an impressive example of putting it all together, from getting clear on strategic intent to revisiting its systems architecture and to reskilling its experienced staff. In terms of strategic intent, this group was focused on ramping up new application development and accelerating its speed to market—meaning faster delivery of innovations to business unit customers within the company. In 2017, it set out to apply intelligent automation to reduce the effort required to develop and deploy new solutions by at least 60 percent. It wanted to see faster deliveries of new capabilities while slashing operating costs by at least half.

With these ambitious goals in mind, managers hosted workshops and hackathons to drum up ideas. After 16 months, they had identified and prioritized different areas using a disciplined opportunity assessment process. To keep work progressing simultaneously along multiple tracks, they established a centralized automation framework and platform to support the entire automation ecosystem and founded a center for excellence to take the journey forward.

Before long, the group could show that it had already saved millions of dollars and been able to redeploy employees to other areas, while making its operations faster and more reliable. This is only the middle of a journey, however, that was mapped through at least 2023. As this company already knows, the journey doesn't end once a well-integrated solution has been deployed. That advantage also has to be sustained.

Recognize Progress

After the successful deployment of automation and the focus turns to the work of sustaining its value, an obvious question arises: What exactly is the value that's been created? The effort started with a certain baseline of costs, performance levels, and products and services. But now some clever solution is in place, so that baseline has changed. The new one is the one to defend—and to use as the next launching point.

So the basic advice here is to measure what matters to the business and document progress, pausing to take stock in a rigorous way of how far the project has come. This assessment should not relate only to how far an organization has come on its automation journey, but also to measure the value or impact that each of the automation solutions or use cases is bringing to the business and its customers. It's especially important to flag cases where that hasn't been achieved, so that managers can take quick action to fix the situation and realize more value. Most companies we know think carefully about the metrics, defining KPIs relating to what they want to achieve with customers and markets, business operations, IT effectiveness, and progress in automation itself.

As an example, think of a health insurer working to automate its customer claims process. Once it rolls out the new solution, it should measure many aspects of performance on a continuous basis. How many users are using the new application? How long does it take for the user to raise a claim through the new application? Is the new application helping the agents sell more products easily? Is the new application stable in terms of performance and are there fewer customer complaints reported? Is the new application saving the targeted effort through automation? These questions all translate into KPIs—for customers, ease of use, market penetration, IT performance, and so on. Chapter 5 stressed the importance of planning the plan. A big part of that is to plan for benefit realization and tracking, which depends on having a robust metrics and measurement system.

Sometimes, the beginnings of this rigorous documentation are already in place in the form of vendor agreements. If a company relies on service providers to perform essential repetitive work, as is often the case with information technology services, it undoubtedly established baseline cost and service levels at the time of contract execution and has tracked them since. These can be updated to reflect the efficiency improvement made along the way.

Documentation of where things stand and what must be sustained isn't only about the outcomes a company is seeing, however. Another aspect of what it has achieved and must maintain is the whole set of building blocks it has put in place to produce those new levels of service and cost reductions: the technologies, the processes, and the knowledge it acquired and built. All of this is subject to erosion and decay if it is not actively maintained. And all this documentation is best done during the course of the automation process and not left until the end. Throughout the automation journey, managers must make the effort not only to track the achievement of interim goals, but also to reflect on what it took to achieve them—and if progress was slower than expected, on what could have been done better.

So documenting achievements is vital, but at the same time it hardly sounds gratifying enough. Leaders should go further and *celebrate* them, and all the innovative work that went into them. This is a point that Chip and Dan Heath emphasize in *Switch: How to Change Things When Change Is Hard*. As that title makes clear, it's a practical book about how to bring about transformation. The authors devote their whole last chapter to the need to "Keep the Switch Going"—or as we would say, to sustain the gains. "The first thing to do," the authors advise, "is recognize and celebrate that first step. Something you've done has worked . . . your team is moving. When you spot movement, you've got to reinforce it." The only problem, they note, is that "most of us are terrible reinforcers." We have to change our own habits to be able to motivate others: "Learning to spot and celebrate approximations requires us to scan the environment constantly, looking for little rays of sunshine, and it isn't easy. Problems are easy to spot; progress, much harder."[2]

Shifting from a mindset of fault-finding to one of appreciation—honoring a job well done—is the best way to provide the inspirational boost for people to stay the course: not only does it produce a sense of satisfaction; it proves that the work is really important to the organization and managers are taking notice. Especially motivating are wins that are described in terms of the positive impacts they produce for employees or customers—for example, in the form of much faster service or greatly reduced frustration. Every high-visibility success helps build trust and enthusiasm for a new round of change.

Rebaseline the Ambition

When we think about the thousands of clients Accenture has worked with on intelligent automation solutions, we often group them in terms of their automation maturity. Some of them we would classify as predigital transformation, as they are still thinking through fundamental twenty-first-century challenges like migrating services to mobile platforms. The majority are in the thick of that digital transformation work. And then there are the minority, perhaps 10 to 20 percent of companies we encounter, that are in the vanguard owing to their investments and experience in automating work.

Our journey metaphor implies that this destination is possible for any organization to reach, but it's also important to keep in mind that not every company aspires to this vanguard position. Some that are at level three in a five-stage maturity model are perfectly satisfied with that level of capability. Some conclude that their business models demand no more than level-two maturity. Sustaining a level of accomplishment entails different activities depending on the level and certainly entails different work than it would take to push to a higher level.

So there is an important question to ask as any substantial automation initiative begins to wind down its development and delivery phase: Will this establish a new status quo that we simply want to maintain? Or having made this achievement and established a new capability in the organization, do we now want to lift our sights higher? In the year to come, are we facing a "sustain" challenge or a "strengthen" one?

The right answer varies with the organization and the circumstances. There is much to be said for overshooting the mark to make sure that, even if some backsliding occurs, the desired level of new capability will still hold. On the other hand, there is the risk of overextending an organization that has only so much capacity to learn and integrate new technologies and ways of working. Part of good management is recognizing when change fatigue is making an impact and people need a chance to catch their breath and consolidate gains.

But another part of good management is maintaining forward motion and always having a plan for preventing an organization from slipping into complacency and falling behind. In the realm of social policy-making, people have often observed that "politics is the art of the possible"—meaning that there may be many things that a given political camp would consider ideal, but its leaders must maintain a very pragmatic focus on what can actually get done, given the constraints and competing agendas of others. The same dynamics exist in large organizations. Internal advocates of intelligent automation might have grand visions of what would constitute a better future of work. They will have to approach that vision in steps, factoring in the constraints they face, even as they keep their eyes on the prize.

Establish a Center of Excellence

Up to now, we have been devoting different chapters to different pieces of the intelligent automation puzzle, addressing ways to overcome the people, process, technology, and strategy issues that organizations face. The important thing to appreciate about any automation success story is that it means all of these have been pulled together and are working as mutually reinforcing elements of a productive system. By the same token, this means that sustaining a success is not simple. All the same elements have to continue to be addressed and kept in a high-performing balance.

This implies the need for an ongoing control and management system—a formal process or mechanism to monitor the performance of solutions in practice and intervene as needed to keep things on track. In turn, that implies that some part of the organization should be accountable for that control and management. It has to be someone's responsibility to keep asking: What operational controls should be in place to ensure that the original problem is still being solved and that other problems haven't developed? And how will we know if the control system itself needs to be adjusted? But, given the role confusion that often exists between IT and the business, this is the kind of responsibility that often slips through the cracks. It isn't obvious who owns the problem.

This may be the most compelling reason for establishing an automation center of excellence (COE; as discussed in Chapter 5). Especially in large organizations, it is easy for automation solutions to proliferate but then to stray off managers' radar screens and fall off organizations' priority lists. The developers involved in designing them migrate to other projects—or other jobs. The workers involved in using them find workarounds when they start to decline in importance. A COE can make up for this by maintaining a current awareness of all the solutions that have been deployed and whether they are still working as desired. It also sustains the organization's automation edge by helping see, based on what all is in place now, how solutions could be improved upon and what opportunities could be targeted next.

Whether or not an organization has set up a COE, it needs to focus on the continued care and feeding of its working solutions—and more broadly, to sustain the momentum of a multiyear journey comprising many automation projects. As tempting as it is to check a box and call a project done, the effort must continue.

Keep Running

The children's classics *Alice's Adventures in Wonderland* and *Through the Looking-Glass*, by Lewis Carroll, contain many famous lines—but for technology professionals, the most memorable is probably the Red Queen's declaration: "Now, here, you see, it takes all the running you can do, to keep in the same place." In the era of machine learning, analytics, AI, and digital workforces, this is certainly true for companies that want to sustain an automation advantage. It is shocking how quickly a leader can find itself playing catchup, and capabilities can turn into liabilities if they are not upgraded on an ongoing basis.

Indeed, it can even be true that a brilliantly conceived solution is obsolete on the day it is launched—if it has taken too long to bring it from the drawing board to reality. This is part of why the concept of continuous development and innovation has spread so quickly across enterprises; fast-changing conditions require not only that development be accelerated but also that it be agile—able to change course in response to real-time feedback and new possibilities. Some of the biggest adopters of continuous development and innovation are the big technology companies such as Amazon, Facebook, Google, and Netflix. These tech giants routinely deploy new features or changes into production not just every day but hundreds or even thousands of times a day.

Automation solutions have been among the fastest evolving of all technologies in the past decade. Take the example of retail. Retail used to be simple. Retailers arrived at shop formats that worked and scaled up by sheer replication, opening more of them. Everything orbited around the shop. Automation was applied to back-end retail operations, like inventory management, where specific tasks performed routinely at high volume cried out for more efficiency, consistency, or transparency. This is what all automation used to be—point solutions and very fragmented. Automation targeted such a pain point in one company and others with the same problem took notice and adopted a solution they saw making impressive productivity improvements at the task level. Yet, automation was not achieving productivity improvements beyond the task level, at a level that would really move the needle on overall business competitiveness.

The evolution that has happened since has not only been about building on that task-level productivity—although that has certainly happened, especially with the introduction of AI to automate some very standard processes completely. Much more consequentially, the evolution has been toward taking these isolated patches of automation and stitching them together into a fabric that stretches across the whole business.

Retail automation started focusing more on the customer interface and how service could be heightened with end-to-end automation. The e-commerce revolution started in earnest in the early 1990s when Netscape launched its first web browser. Then very quickly, Pizza Hut gave customers the opportunity to order online, and eBay was able to offer shoppers a whole new kind of marketplace."

It is in this reconceived model of the enterprise that digital tools have increasingly been recognized to have more than just productivity benefits. To frame automation as simply taking away well-defined tasks from people who used to perform them is to severely constrain the potential benefits to be gained from it. As companies now enter their post-digital-transformation era, many are taking off the blinders that kept them from seeing possibilities beyond the productivity benefits of operational cost savings. Retailers, for example, now have new ways to study customer behavior, understand purchasing patterns, personalize

offers, and transform the shopping experience. In other industries, companies are imagining their own opportunities for
previously impossible competitive differentiations and enhanced
customer experiences.

We've come a long way in a very short period of time. Does
it make sense to expect this trend to grind to a halt in the years
to come? More likely, the pace of change will continue to accelerate. Just to sustain the competitive advantages they have made
with intelligent automation, companies will have to continuously push forward, pursuing next-generation possibilities. It
will take all of their imagination to do this, so they must keep
engaging their people with innovation exercises like hackathons
and design thinking workshops. They will keep harvesting ideas
through "voice of the customer" and employee idea jams, and
invest in disciplined processes to scan for new developments in
intelligent automation technologies and their applications in
different commercial sectors. To stay in the same place, they will
need to keep running.

Grow Your Talent

As obvious as this statement is, it has to be said: an organization can't sustain a change effort without continuing to fund
it. Automation initiatives must have resources to keep going
strong. But the vagaries of corporate budgeting sometimes leave
them starving and unable to continue moving forward.

The resources required are, fundamentally, financial investments, but they go to support capabilities more fundamental
than the things that can be obtained with purchase orders. The
biggest paybacks come from longer-term investments in human
capabilities. Jack Chua, director of data science at the online

travel agent Expedia, puts it this way: "If you decide to build something in-house, it's hard to find a deep learning expert or a machine learning expert that can maintain it over time. What this means is that your business has to be mature enough to support these engineers."[3]

Even for those intelligent automation solutions that are provided by vendors, the resource requirement remains. Chua notes that "a lot of people have a notion that, once they build it for me, it's done—I have the capability. In reality, it's something that needs to be maintained over time and improved" because, for example, "bugs can pop up." No solution is perfect, he stresses, and that means, "from a strategic perspective, or a technical perspective, you have to think about it as a long-term investment versus a 'build and throw it over the fence.'"

It's an important reminder that intelligent automation is not an event but a process—and most of all, a journey.

Keep Governance Engaged

In every automation initiative we have seen succeed at scale, governance has been a big part of the effort. If a team pulled together the right level of overseers, representing the right mix of stakeholders, it gained many benefits. They asked the hard questions, ensured alignment with the larger strategic goals of the enterprise, helped problem solve, ran interference where necessary, and functioned as automation advocates and champions. It's important to recognize, however, that they too are only human. Like others whose attention is required to get automation to take hold and yield long-term returns, they can be distracted by other pressing concerns. They may be tempted to shift their attention to new priorities. On the automation front, they may be ready to declare "mission accomplished."

To help keep everyone focused on the automation journey, it helps to establish a structure with all stakeholders that enables intelligent tracking, reporting, and governance for all intelligent automation initiatives. Stakeholders should represent multiple organizational functions, including the business, IT, finance, and human resources. The governance structure should clearly define authority, decision-making responsibilities, execution ownership, oversight requirements, stakeholder alignment, and risk management approaches to ensure the automation is consistent, scalable, and delivering the expected value to the enterprise. There should be regular meetings, evaluations, and escalation points aligned to the intelligent automation strategy to ensure the holistic implementation of automation. In addition, the structure should provide for a continuous feedback channel and communication between the business and IT group.

Effective automation project leaders don't make the mistake of taking their advisory groups for granted. They keep them feeling highly invested in the success of the effort. One manager told us her approach was to "figure out what makes their role fulfilling and enjoyable and add to those parts. Find out which aspects annoy, depress, or bore them to tears, and eliminate whatever you can of those elements." How would a project manager find all this out? The easy advice is to ask them.

One of the most contentious areas for a governance group, for example, can be its most important task: sorting out decision rights so that decisions are made with maximum clarity and minimum delay, while drawing on the right set of inputs. Often, it is not obvious which decisions can be left to a project team and which need to be brought to executives. Nothing slows down a team's efforts more than ambiguity about who gets to decide on a critical-path matter.

Another cause of friction can be how agendas are structured, and how much time is allocated to discussing, for example, different forms of project risk and how to manage them. And governance bodies can also be afflicted with all the usual inter-personal issues that get in the way of team effectiveness: clashing personalities, conflicting communication styles, and diverging views of what a successful project looks like.

It may seem that the effective collaboration of the gover-nance body is out of scope for a project-level manager to judge or try to improve. The truth is that, more than almost anything, this will affect the long-term sustainability of the solution the project delivers—so to leave it to fate cannot really be an option. Just like a chief executive in relation to a corporate board of directors, anyone leading an automation effort needs to manage up even as they are being managed—and part of that upward management should be aimed at increasing engagement.

Make Improvement Continuous

While much of governance activity is focused on the automa-tion program itself, the broader automation landscape should also be subject to tight monitoring and robust control. As orga-nizations mature and transition to new business models, they will invariably undertake a growing number of automation and AI implementations to support their transformations. To operationalize these at faster speed and create greater long-term business value, managers will need to apply leading practices. Yet, with the world of AI and automation continuously chang-ing, the practices around delivery management that count as leading are in a constant state of flux. AI technology evolves at such a fast pace that old practices quickly become outdated and are replaced by new ones. Meanwhile, continuous monitoring of the applications is necessary to avoid performance deviations, redundant applications, and underused applications—and to ensure that a continuous stream of value is created by the end-to-end automation journey.

Innovate to Sharpen Your Competitive Edge

Paul Daugherty, who leads technology efforts at Accenture as group chief executive – technology and chief technology officer, likes to say that "there's no finish line for innovation." A company might be well ahead of the pack in how it solves an important problem, but it can't afford to ease up because the race will only go on. To help fuel innovation, businesses should:

- Keep identifying new areas to create enhanced customer experiences, drive incremental value from its existing operations, and accelerate growth.
- Actively incubate and prototype new concepts that will have near-term impacts on the business. Encourage the contribution of ideas and innovation-harvesting through an innovation council.
- Invest in the trends research and thought leadership capacity to identify and anticipate game-changing business, market, and technology developments. This isn't only an imperative for companies traditionally thought of as creative or consultative businesses. It drives greater success in any growing business.

- Partner with and invest in growth-stage companies that create innovative enterprise technologies using an open innovation approach.
- Invest in learning and development at all levels of the organization.

Continue to Lead Change

We previously mentioned John Kotter's work on change management, and now is a good time to consider how it applies to sustaining an automation advantage in particular. In his classic book *Leading Change*, Kotter lays out an eight-part model for moving an organization firmly into a new state of being:

1. Create a *sense of urgency*: Have an answer to "why now?"
2. Form a *powerful coalition* to guide the effort.
3. Create a *vision for positive change*.
4. *Communicate* that vision in compelling ways.
5. *Empower action broadly* in the organization.
6. Create *quick wins*: Generate momentum early.
7. Build on the change: *Don't let up.*
8. Make it stick in the organizational *culture*.

He breaks this eight-step model into three major phases. In fact, to us, the essential insight of Kotter's model is that the change itself—the communication of what needs to change, the broad set of actions taken, and the immediate proof points achieved that he lists as steps 4, 5, and 6—is just one phase, central, but not sufficient. It must be sandwiched by a lot of work to first motivate the organization to want to change and later, to keep it from backsliding.

Kotter's seventh step, "Build on the change," recognizes the truth that we have been trying to communicate here: that sustaining often demands strengthening. Overshooting the mark helps: it can ensure that, even with some backsliding, the progress will be on target. Ideally, it will mean much more is accomplished than was planned. In Kotter's words, "Instead of declaring victory, leaders of successful efforts use the credibility afforded by short-term wins to tackle even bigger problems." They extend the vision of the original transformation to new frontiers. They notice the people skills that went into the success and set to work developing and spreading those more broadly throughout the workforce. They take on projects with broader scope than the early ones. "They understand that renewal efforts take not months but years."[4]

In the end, as this classic model shows, the mark of a successful project is whether it sticks, and that will not be known for some time. For it to happen, the change needs to take hold in the very culture of the enterprise, at a much deeper level than its processes, policies, and procedures. If it seeps into the level of norms and values, it can have a self-sustaining quality that will keep people adhering to the new system even when no direct pressure is being applied to get them to do so.

People can embrace a new way of working, a new system and set of relationships between human and machine labor, if they see clear evidence that it changes things for the better. This is largely a matter of communication around the theory of the change. That is, communications must not only hold up the impressive positive results, but also clearly connect the dots between cause and effect. The whole organization must see that it was the introduction of the automation solution, as opposed to other changes that might have taken place in the same timeframe, that directly drove the happy outcome.

Finally, for change to take hold in the culture, people must see their bosses, all the way up the line, not just as committed to the change, but as models of it. If the hope is that an organization will be full of frontline employees spotting new opportunities for automation of tasks they perform, then it is vital that those employees see their managers doing the same with regard to managerial tasks. Even more fundamentally, top leadership should be visibly committed to data-driven decision making. Mariya Yao is a chief technology officer at an enterprise AI company and also heads up TOPBOTS, a publication and community for enterprise AI professionals. She says:

> There is no point in laboriously gathering data and running sophisticated machine learning models if the analysis will be ignored. Many of the world's largest enterprises have historically grown through gut decisions from influential executives, not from collaborative, data-driven decision-making. Due to past successes, some leaders prioritize their own beliefs and methods and are openly hostile to analytic approaches and centralized technology.[5]

No automation journey will go far, she believes, if the corporate culture does not value data and analytics in the first place.

Secure the Commitment of Management

The ranks of executive leadership should consist of true believers—and if they are not that today, the next round of successions should ensure that a next generation of automation-savvy leadership is installed. Executives have limited attention and a huge amount of discretion in what they prioritize. Commitment to intelligent automation must start at the top-level management.

At Amazon, for example, founder Jeff Bezos has long required that the executives leading the company's major lines of business prepare clear, six-page narratives every year, setting forth their business plans. While the content of these narratives is as different as the businesses themselves—which range from Amazon Web Services to Whole Foods grocery operations— every one of them features an answer to one question: How are you planning to use machine learning?[6]

When a CEO really cares about gaining an edge with a particular capability, this is how it shows. It doesn't stray off their radar screen. Anything less will result in suboptimal behavior that can erode the automation program, especially when the focus is enterprisewide automation implementation. With a lack of commitment from the top management, decisions on investment priorities and talent transformation may lag as everyone will have different priorities on which to focus. While many will give lip service to capabilities that would be nice to have, gaining an automation advantage depends on a top management team that considers it essential.

Bristol Myers Squibb's Intelligent Automation Journey

Bristol Myers Squibb (BMS), the global biopharmaceutical company, launched an initiative in 2017 to gain efficiencies and productivity by scaling intelligent automation throughout the enterprise. To this end, it created four integrated COEs—for Lean digital, cloud computing, DevOps, and Agile—each of which has an innovation framework focused on discovering, ideating, incubating, and operationalizing intelligent automation solutions for various functions to reduce technical debt and free up funds for business development. The COEs interact with each other to identify opportunities for intelligent automation, develop IT solutions, and maximize value through proof of concept.

Within the first two years of its intelligent automation journey, BMS has automated numerous complex manual processes to eliminate inefficiencies, improve productivity, and solve pain points in key business units, including clinical, finance, HR, procurement, and supply chain. For example, it has eliminated 92,000 hours of manual effort, accelerated the software development life cycle by 40 percent, and reduced ticket volume by more than 20 percent. To do this, the COEs have leveraged intelligent automation tools such as robotic process automation bots, automated ticket resolution, and self-healing applications; employed modern engineering practices, such as full-stack DevOps; and effected culture change through design thinking, continuous innovation, and cocreation. In short, its COE-driven intelligent automation initiative has given BMS a structured, comprehensive approach for managing automation across the enterprise and achieving business-aligned IT innovation, as well as faster and less expensive application management and software development.

As a result of its success, BMS continues to expand enterprise intelligent automation by investing in AI labs to focus on AI proofs of concept and scaled adoption. BMS has also started building cognitive robotic process automation bots and driving culture and talent transformation with full-stack automation engineering. Through these initiatives, BMS continues to expand the use of intelligent automation across the company.

Key Takeaways

▶ An intelligent automation solution is not a "set it and forget it" accomplishment. Once a project wraps up, managers must avoid the temptation to declare victory and move on to the next initiative.

▶ Even when solutions work as first implemented, they are always possible to improve. Sustaining the gains means tracking their operations and outcomes and tweaking them based on feedback data.

▶ Managers must also anticipate the atrophy that naturally occurs as the broader technology and business environment in which a solution was designed to operate continues to evolve.

▶ At the highest level, organizations must keep looking for new ways to exploit the power of intelligent automation. Leaders must continue to inject fresh energy to sustain the momentum toward applying it at scale.

Relevance, Resilience, and Responsibility

I n many books, the final chapter is devoted to summarizing what has already been said and underscoring the overall message the authors want to convey. We're happy to devote at least a paragraph to that: the whole message of this book is that this is a key moment in the emergence of a new class of technologies when the right approach to applying them can make all the difference.

Many enterprises today—commercial enterprises, nonprofit organizations, and government agencies—are experimenting and investing in intelligent automation. Yet they are not achieving the full value of these potentially transformative capabilities. Those that do make the leap to scale will gain an enduring performance advantage. All the advice we have offered in previous chapters has been about gaining that automation edge.

Resolving to gain that edge, however, is as much a question of embracing the right management principles as it is about investing in the right technologies. Our preference, then, is to devote this last chapter to the ideals to strive for during an automation initiative, however small it starts and however big it scales. The convenient shorthand we offer is that automation solutions must be relevant, resilient, and responsible. As guideposts for decision-making these may sound unsurprising—even obvious, perhaps. But we refer to them as ideals because in most organizations, there is still a long way to go in all three respects.

Relevance

There is a classic tension in all realms of scientific progress that comes down to this: the experts driving the leading-edge work tend to be captivated by intellectually interesting challenges, while the people in a position to apply discoveries and inventions are consumed by very real-world, practical problems. Often there is a wide gulf between the state of the art and the needs of the market. Let's call it the relevance gap—and let's recognize that it is a problem in intelligent automation, too.

Developers of automation solutions might pride themselves on their cutting-edge technology stack, or the elegance of their AI algorithms, but if their customers—inside or outside the organization—can't see the value in them or get that value to materialize in practice, the achievement in business terms is irrelevant.

It's important to stress, at the same time, that relevance is a fast-moving target. Technology has advanced rapidly in the past decade, and there is no reason to expect the pace of change to slow down in the foreseeable future. The ways that consumers interact with their surroundings are also changing quickly with the widespread introduction of advanced automation and AI.

New consumer preferences are forming and baseline expectations are rising. Businesses today face a real challenge, therefore, to remain relevant in a world that is constantly changing. Will their automation efforts see them setting the pace for others or struggling to keep up?

One truth can never be ignored: relevance is in the eye of the beholder. It can only be assessed from the perspective of the customer. Understanding the relevance of an initiative therefore requires capturing and interpreting customer expectations and customer satisfaction. This calls for both quantitative and qualitative analysis, since it is famously hard for customers to identify the need for a solution in a form they have never encountered before.

A business such as Apple may come along occasionally, determined to reshape market expectations with offerings customers never knew they wanted. Most businesses will have to work hard to create a culture that innovates in accordance with the changing expectations of the customer. The most relevant solution for someone with a problem to solve is not the barely sufficient one they have used in the past, but the better one that will come next.

Take this to a point of individualized problems and solutions, and it's easy to envision an explosion of personalized products and services. This is the vision of mass customization. We've already mentioned the exciting realm of personalized medicine—but tailoring to the individual consumer will hardly stop there. Think of something as simple as footwear. Right now, shoes are somewhat customizable, with some manufacturers like Nike allowing online customers to specify designs online, but the variable elements are superficial ones, mainly having to do with colors, embroidery, or stenciling. Imagine the shoe of the future, custom built to a three-dimensional portrait of your foot. As such offerings begin to proliferate, consumer demand will rise for them in additional areas, and personalized and AI-enhanced products and services will become common.

Few industries are more focused on relevance than the fashion industry, so perhaps it's no surprise that we find exciting examples of relevant automation there. Clothing and apparel brands are constantly looking for the next better way to get their goods in front of buyers and create awareness and demand in the market. Increasingly, they are using machine learning and other AI strengths to uplift users' shopping experience and improve the efficiency of sales systems. Customer assistance is being taken to new levels by predictive analytics and guided sales processes. Fashion brands are also starting to leverage conversational assistants through chatbots and voice assistant devices such as Amazon Alexa, Apple Siri, Google Home, and Microsoft Cortana. Using conversational interfaces, fashion brands can ask customers questions and find the patterns in customer desires and trends. Combining awareness of past purchases and other data sources, they can suggest add-on accessories and related items. A customer seeking a new dress or pair of shoes, instead of searching through a website or mobile app, can simply have a conversation with an intelligent conversational agent. Through dialogue, the customer arrives at that must-have next purchase. Meanwhile, the interaction has been more satisfying for the customer and much more valuable for the fashion brand.[1]

For an automation team itself to clear the relevance bar, the team must be close enough to customers to appreciate the pain points they would love to resolve—and creative enough to work on them. Setting aside long-standing assumptions and ingrained approaches is essential, whether the problem is framed as developing a more compelling and attractive customer experience or overhauling an entire business model. When management gurus talk about the need for solutions that are future-proof—one of today's biggest buzzwords—they are really talking about relevance.

An automation solution should be, from both the technology and business angles, far enough ahead of the curve that it will not be subject to immediate obsolescence as the world continues to change. And yet it will not be so futuristic that it cannot be put to productive use immediately. Relevance depends on appreciating what, in the customer's mind, constitutes an important—but manageable—step ahead of their competition.

For technology teams, the relevance imperative means a need for greater agility in software deployment. Solutions aren't worth much if they are designed and developed too late to solve pressing problems. Fast-build practices like Agile need to be adopted and become second nature. The speed with which new designs or growth initiatives go to market decides whether the business will stay ahead of the competition or not. A business might have the most innovative solution, but if the release gets delayed, its faster competitor might seize the opportunity with a similar one, even if it is not as good.

Consider the mea culpa issued recently by one group of top executives in an investor relations call. Compelled to address yet another year of declining unit sales in the company's main line of products, the executives chalked it up to not improving the product lineup fast enough. They specifically cited longer development and design lead times and poor product planning and development as two causes for the slower pace.

Speed is all the more important in a global economy that is more and more platform oriented.[2] We know that in any networked system, the value of the network, and therefore the platform supporting it, is directly proportional to the number of people using it. The earliest innovators in a situation where there is a platform opportunity are often able to establish advantages that followers find next to impossible to overcome. Once the new platform attracts a critical mass of participants, its adoption curve hits an elbow inflection point, after which growth is exponential.

Given these increasing returns to scale, it isn't enough to get a well-designed offering into the market—it needs to get to market fast and ideally first.[3] For some traditionally managed businesses, this perspective will force deep change to entire internal operations. New ways of thinking and working will be required to embrace transformative change as a constant, energizing process and not a rare and wrenching occurrence.

Resilience

Resilience is key to the sustained vitality of a business—strategic resilience, operational resilience, and systems resilience. At all these levels it means the ability to recover from disruptions large and small, and to keep operating through crisis with minimal impact on critical business and operational processes. At the foundation of most businesses' overall resilience is the resilience of their information systems. This is because, especially in today's digitized world, every business is fundamentally an information business.

Unfortunately, too many systems today are highly brittle, not up to the challenge of adapting to shifting conditions. Intelligent automation can play a pivotal role in changing that, allowing companies to navigate through dynamic and complex situations. Indeed, AI's ability to learn fast and course correct can even mean that weathering a crisis leaves an enterprise *more* capable than before—an appealing prospect for every business operating in conditions of uncertainty and volatility.[4] Intelligent automation can make the systems driving business self-healing and self-maintaining, run business applications unattended, assist customers with queries through automation, and enable workforces to be productive in virtual environments.

As we work on this chapter, the world remains in lockdown due to the Covid-19 pandemic. In the midst of this healthcare and economic crisis, enterprises struggle to protect the health and safety of their people. They also need to ensure the stability of critical business operations and underlying systems. Many employers are regretting the fact that more had not been done to ensure their systems' ability to operate during a major disruption or crisis, with minimal impact on critical business and processes. In this unfolding crisis, systems resilience is being tested like never before—on a global scale, with companies reeling from work stoppages and struggling to recover and mitigate their impact.

In Chapter 6, we discussed architecting automation to be adaptive—equipping systems with the self-awareness and autonomy to learn, improve, and adapt by themselves. For example, if one chatbot goes down, a monitoring function can immediately note that performance has suffered and proceed to repair or replace it. If a customer faces an issue in placing an order, even before that shopper places a call to customer care, an adaptive automated system can detect the problem and immediately trigger a corrective action. The self-healing happens in minutes. An app that interfaces with others can update itself when a change is necessary. Imagine, for example, that a certain step called for the app to schedule a call via a particular telecom platform, but the company now favors a different platform. Another example is utilities companies that use network sensors and devices to monitor the flow of, say, water or electricity. Intelligent automation means that these devices need not be constrained by the set of rules that were in place when they were first deployed. Along the way, they gain understanding of the factors that drive usage and based on that understanding can alter the functioning of the grid in real time to achieve higher performance.

It is easy to recognize how automation with more self-healing and predictive capabilities dramatically lowers the effort required of operations support staff in a situation requiring resilience—allowing them to focus on other aspects of a challenge. Adaptivity means that intelligent systems using machine learning are able to form predictions, observe outcomes, and then make adjustments based on this feedback to improve their predictions in the next round. Adaptable systems respond to changing requirements and environments and in doing so empower people to decide and act in the face of uncertainty. Key markers of adaptable organizations include enterprisewide use of automation and AI, a continuous data supply chain in the cloud to power AI in the enterprise, and an architecture that is stable yet modular, flexible, decoupled, and constantly evolving.

An important impact of these highly adaptable systems is that they bring new levels of resilience to organizations. In fact, as increasingly interconnected companies gain a new appreciation of the risks of disruption, we see the entire motivation behind automation efforts changing. It used to be that the point of automation was simply to perform routine tasks in a more efficient and standardized way. Increasingly, a top reason to automate is to create an operating system that allows a company to turn on a dime.

This is why, when the Covid-19 pandemic hit in early 2020, it did not take long to see enterprises getting more serious about their automation investments. *TechRepublic*, for example, reported Forrester industry analyst Leslie Joseph saying: "Pre-Covid-19 automation efforts were often stalled because of automation sprawl, because different parts of a company experimented with automation in isolation, with disparate standards, which failed to attain scale. However, with automation becoming a top-down boardroom initiative, we expect greater stewardship and oversight of a firm's automation efforts."[5] The reason, in our view, has everything to do with resilience.

Even before the coronavirus began making an impact, Accenture was researching what makes some companies more resilient than others and how that benefits them. In a broad-based survey of enterprises, we scored their relative resilience based on two proxy measures: their levels of technology adoption and organizational flexibility. The crisis provided a stark lesson in how important these are to organizational survival. It laid bare the need to understand and address systems vulnerabilities and provide for greater resilience.

Many companies will now build competencies they wish they'd invested in before: to be more digital, data-driven, and in the cloud; to have more variable cost structures, agile operations, and automation; and to create stronger capabilities in e-commerce and security. As they go about building long-term capabilities, they will now be much more oriented toward the need for adaptability and agility in response to unforeseen, potentially catastrophic developments. Our hope as economies start to reopen is that managers will take their first steps with an eye to the larger transformation their organizations will need. *Reopening* can also be a program of *reinvention*.

"Enterprises across the world are watching as large segments of their human workforce and human-driven value chains are suspended," Joseph says. "As we emerge from the crisis, firms will look to automation as a way to mitigate the risks that future crises pose to the supply and productivity of human workers." Expect to see greater investment in the intelligent automation toolkit—the cognitive capabilities of applied AI, industrial robotics, service robots, and robotic process automation.

Responsibility

The third major principle that must guide future human-and-machine pairing is responsibility: a much greater level of attention to the ethical issues raised by these powerful new tools. Machines, left to their own devices, have no ethos to guide them. As for people, there is nothing more differentiating about the human race than its capacity for moral action—and nothing more disappointing than someone's setting their morals aside.

Among those who are wary of the advancing capabilities of AI, the worst fears are about irresponsible applications and dangerous misuses of it. Beyond the threats of job destruction, the possibilities range from deepfakes spreading misinformation to unprecedented surveillance tools empowering totalitarian repression. In China, for example, Baidu's Deep Voice software can clone a voice based on just 3.7 seconds of audio input from the original.[6] The appealing side of this is that, for example, you could choose to have a novel read to you in any voice, from the author's own to your late grandmother's. You could have your favorite actress telling you the next turn to take as you use a navigation app. At the same time, the potential for abuse is obvious.

Ethics will come to the fore with increasing violations of privacy, biases in decision-making, and lack of control over automated systems and robots. And solutions to ethics issues will have to be scalable, as intelligent automation becomes ever more widely applied, more deeply embedded in customer solutions, and more responsible for decisions that affect lives—such as medical diagnoses, government benefit payments, and mortgage approvals. Legal scholars are already busy identifying the issues that will inevitably arise and proposing frameworks and principles for dealing with them consistently.[7] Four of these principles are certain to remain pillars of "responsible automation." To avoid causing reckless or heedless damage, solutions will have to be unbiased, transparent, controllable, and protected.

Unbiased Decisions

An intelligent automation solution is only as good as its data. Particularly when AI is embedded in an intelligent automation solution, it becomes clear how the characteristics of the data used to train an AI model influence the recommendations and decisions it produces. An infamous example was an AI-powered chatbot named Tay, created by a team of researchers and given its own social media account.

Of course, the bot wasn't coded to be racist, a *TechCrunch* journalist reported—it just learned from the other accounts it interacted with. "And naturally, given that this is the internet, one of the first things online users taught Tay was how to be racist, and how to spout back ill-informed or inflammatory political opinions."[8]

More often, an enterprise AI solution is trained on a data set largely consisting of proprietary records of customer profiles, interactions, and transactions. But this, too, can easily allow the tool to spot and act on patterns that drive its recommendations and decisions in ways that cause harm to groups of people. Sometimes this is because the nature of data is always that it is historical—it may not represent the current reality well enough to predict likely outcomes in the future. Sometimes it is because the output of the decision-making process itself adds up to a pattern of discrimination that the company never intended—and which creates legal exposure for the company and often mortifying reputational damage.

Already there have been widely condemned examples of racial and gender bias patterns in business AI use. Vivienne Ming describes in the *Financial Times*, for example, the terrible surprise that a technology company's human resources executives had when they tried to use AI to find the best candidates in the mountain of résumés the company receives. Having trained it on the backgrounds of people who had succeeded in challenging technology jobs in the past, they were dismayed when the candidates it selected were overwhelmingly male. Avoiding such an outcome isn't just a matter of having unbiased AI developers, or even better data, Ming insists. There also have to be people and processes focused on de-biasing the data (as the company learned and quickly put in place).[9]

One of the oldest and truest sayings in the information systems world is "garbage in, garbage out" (GIGO). The output of a system will never be useful if the input was fatally flawed from the start. In the realm of AI, there is a version of GIGO we might call BIBO: bias in, bias out. When these high-profile embarrassments occur for companies and the work is done to unpack how the machinery could have come up with such results, usually the problem can be traced to the base data itself. Since most of the data points are collecting the actions of humans in real-world scenarios—choices they have made, experiences they have had—the human biases, often implicit and acting on a subconscious level, end up tainting the AI models' training.

The effect, then, of the AI solution's application is to amplify and magnify the bias. To the extent possible, it is imperative to identify and eliminate the potential for bias before training the

AI model. Even if care is taken to do this, however, there must also be ex post facto assessments to flag the problem if outputs are unfairly weighted for or against people with characteristics that really should not matter to the decision at hand.

There are statistical methods that can be adopted to minimize the data bias. There are also good management processes to reduce bias in an AI model. Here are several tips to keep in mind:

- Identify the bias vectors an AI model is exposed to, among them the ethical, social, political, and historical biases that could infect its training.
- Gather perspectives from experts in varied fields about possible negative scenarios that should be anticipated and avoided. Establish metrics to monitor any movement toward or away from these scenarios.
- Vet the data for its inclusiveness and ability to represent the full diversity of the population, across gender, race, ethnicity, religion, ideology, and other social lines.
- Know the data so thoroughly that it's easy to focus on and quickly fix any problematic tags. Structure the data well.
- Identify and neutralize any factors that can be foreseen or identified in practice as driving outcomes in prejudiced and discriminatory directions.
- Continuously analyze performance and outcomes, and incorporate feedback from users.

Of course, the point is not to eliminate all bias from AI, even if that were practically possible. AI's ability to find and act on patterns that humans' own cognitive biases or limited perspective have kept hidden is central to its value. The problem emerges when the biases that AI tends toward are socially unjust based on historical patterns that society has rejected. The infamous examples of bias in AI have all had to do with situations where the AI's output is perpetuating a discriminatory stance, and using the AI would actively undermine the progress that humanity is trying to make. At a level higher than the previous bullet points, we can offer a handful of management approaches that we have seen organizations use to eliminate bias in their intelligent automation solutions.

Break Major Business Problem Areas Down into Manageable Segments

Addressing any major area that is inherently problematic in terms of bias forces a team to imagine a wide range of scenarios and anticipate all the ways that stereotypes could influence algorithms across multiple system modules. Scoping an initial target for a solution more narrowly will make it easier to comprehend its complexity and trace the origins of any unintended consequences, while also raising the likelihood that it will perform efficiently and satisfy the need it was built to serve.

Empathize with End Users in Development

A good way to make a model more user friendly is to adopt the points of view of many kinds of people who will use it and be affected by it. Do this personally and as a team, actively role-playing and challenging decisions as a devil's advocate, to avoid being surprised by an AI bias that end users might face as they interact with the model.

Subject the Model to Diverse Testers

At the launch phase of a model, expose it to as diverse a group as possible and to experts in AI bias avoidance. Understand that an AI response that one person considers to be purely rational and neutral can be perceived by another set of people as deeply biased. The more viewpoints in the room, the more problems can be avoided. As well as detecting potential for bias in this model, the others' input will guide better planning for more bias-free models in the future.

Create Feedback Systems That Recognize Diversity

If a model has a diverse set of people interacting with it and being affected by it, then it would be a lost opportunity if feedback systems managed to erase that diversity by emphasizing only the model's overall performance. Introduce ways of getting and considering more nuanced feedback. More fine-grained information will reveal if certain segments of people are having experiences different from the majority (and possibly becoming frustrated that their voices are not being heard).

Establish a System of Continuous Improvement Based on Feedback

Have a process in place by which the model will continue to be tweaked based on feedback received. This will allow the model to continuously move toward the ideal of unbiased, accurate performance. Remember that once deployed, AI models are exposed to various scenarios and circumstances. Even the highest level of due diligence cannot guarantee complete elimination of bias.

Create Transparent Systems

In his revelatory book *Principles*, Bridgewater Associates founder Ray Dalio devotes some words to describing his company's pioneering use of automation in investment decision-making—a process where, he says, "the machine does most of the work and we interact with it in a quality way." He writes:

One of the great things about algorithmic decision making is that it focuses people on cause-effect relationships and, in that way, helps foster a real idea meritocracy. When everyone can see the criteria algorithms use and have a hand in developing them, they can all agree that the system is fair and trust the computer to look at the evidence, make the right assessments about people, and assign them the right authorities. The algorithms are essentially principles in action on a continuous basis.[10]

What Dalio is describing is what more designers of automation solutions should aim for. In most cases, automation and intelligence technology are more like a black box. People may see the inputs and they can easily see the results, but they don't have a clue about the weightings and calculations of the algorithms being used or the logic of the decision-making process.

This brings us to the concept of explainable AI, often referred to as XAI.[11] These are systems that can explain the steps in their decision-making process, the alternatives involved, and how they arrived at an output. This gives a fair idea of the behavioral patterns of the technology and how its future evolution paths can be mapped. As a result, the technology becomes more transparent and has a built-in trust factor.

In today's world, AI algorithms are being applied to highly sensitive territory, such as in legal affairs and medical diagnostics. In areas like these, where the costs of mistakes can be very high, automated decision-making will be subjected to even greater scrutiny in years to come. Imagine the extreme, hypothetical situation of AI standing in for a judge and jury. Once the AI finds a defendant guilty and renders its decision as to punishment, what if the defendant files an appeal, asking a higher court to reverse the decision? In that case, the higher court's first step is to investigate the decision-making process used in the first round. But if the lower court's AI system is a typical black box, that investigation goes nowhere, and the higher court must reconsider the case by its own logic. Now imagine that using its own preferred logic the higher court overturns the verdict. With that reversal, the credibility of the AI system is damaged; it got the answer wrong evidently, and there is no clear way to adjust it to get things more right in the future. Growing distrust eventually leads to abandonment of the AI system.

By analogy, this kind of situation is easier to imagine in the realm of medical diagnostics, where AI is already making significant inroads. Any diagnosis indicated by an AI system is carefully reviewed by a physician before a therapy or intervention is prescribed to the patient. If the experienced judgment of the human doctor does not match the data-driven diagnosis of the AI, the doctor gets the final say—but the doctor will want to review why the AI came to a different conclusion. If the AI systems are opaque, doctors will go with their own judgment, both because they have more confidence in it and because they can explain the reasoning to their patients. Again, having done so once, a doctor is less likely in a similar situation to use the AI system for the initial diagnostic, having lost faith in its usefulness. No change in behavior will take hold, and whoever decided to invest in this AI diagnostic system will see the implementation fail.

There can be multiple such situations where an explanation might be needed from an AI system to validate its decisions. A car insurance company will probably want to review the decision-making process of a driverless car before settling the insurance claim. A university's admissions department might be under scrutiny if it suddenly rejects the applications of a group of students that happens to be of a particular ethnic origin. The decision-making might have been entirely on merit considerations, but regulatory authorities will probably want to take a deeper look at the decision process. As such, AI systems of the future cannot remain opaque if they have to garner trust from their human users. Without trust, the implementation of AI systems will remain incomplete and will not be able to reach its full potential.

Since the advent of the intelligence technologies, the scientific communities are constantly trying to come up with solutions that can explain the decision-making process of the machines. In the earlier decades when machines used to work on a limited number of hard-coded rule-based algorithms, the detection for the most dominant combination of rules behind any decision was relatively easy. Today, with the advent of the neural networks and genetic algorithms, the tracking of the entire decision flow has become far more difficult. However, the scientists are coming up with methods like layerwise relevance propagation (LRP) for determining the most dominant parameter of an input vector resulting in a specific decision.

Various AI technologies are being developed to bring about varying degrees of interpretability to the decision-making process. The degree of interpretability may vary in accordance to the criticality of the system. A lot of research is going on to maintain known algorithms like decision trees and Bayesian classifiers as the foundation of the decision algorithm of the AI systems. Using known algorithms helps increase trust in the decisions of an intelligent system.

Despite all these efforts there will probably never be a perfect solution to the black box problem. The source of the problem is intertwined with the technology that makes AI systems so effective. Work to mitigate the effects will remain as work-in-progress. If we rely on a machine using deep neural networks as the basis of decision-making, its power comes from the fact that the outcome cannot be attributed to the functionalities of any one neuron. It is the combination of many such neurons and interconnectivity between the layers that gives rise to the resulting outcome.

Although it might be possible to find the dominant input vector, building an entire chain of decision flow would be a daunting task. Then there is the problem arising out of dimensionality, if the intelligence technology is using support vector machines, commonly known as SVM technology. Human beings are incapable of identifying the plane of data segregation into a decision tree if more than three variables are used. Here, we have used the word "plane" a bit loosely to drive the point; it effectively stands for two-dimensional variable structure. If the intelligence system is advanced enough to use, say, 20 such variables while segregating the decision plane, it will never be humanly possible to visualize such a multidimensional point of reference.

Controllable Actions

As the intelligent automation technology progresses, identifying the decision flow will become more and more difficult. If the scientists are adding more neurons or dimensions to the incumbent AI technology, it will drastically increase the complexity of interpreting the decision-making process. Even localized interpretations will no longer be feasible. The only other way to help make the AI more responsible is to add a certain degree of human control on the entire decision flow.[12] Therefore, a closer look at the feasibilities and efficiencies of a human-in-loop kind of system is warranted. In this system, the entire decision system will be built around intervening human inputs at critical checkpoints, which can alter the course of the decision process.

To better understand this system of built-in human control, let us take the example of automated weapons systems. The weapons systems can be trained to identify so-called bogeys automatically based on various factors. However, if these systems can actually attack automatically without any human control, they may kill innocents. Such a border protection system may automatically go on high alert if some unknown entity trespasses into the territories of a nation, but it has no or limited ways to differentiate between a refugee and an infiltrator. Even in combat situations, autonomous systems are less likely to follow international rules of engagement or other such contextual factors like the tenets of the Geneva Conventions. Having a human being in control of such systems is a must.

The ultimate target of designing systems with the built-in human factor is to bring in an element of traceability. Just like any other technology, the international community will have to build regulatory frameworks around intelligent automation systems. Such frameworks can only work if there is an element of accountability and ownership. Therefore, the post facto investigations and reviews must lead to at least one human being or one human organization or government. Then there is the matter of establishing intent in any such proceeding. Establishing the intent of a machine is an impossible task—and therefore, decoupling a machine from any human intervention absolves it of harboring malicious or magnanimous intent. It takes away the whole concept of responsibility and accountability with it.

Therefore, bringing in a human control element in the decision-making process will not only ensure retracing the steps of the decision-making process but also ensure that the steps get tracked in run time. The human inputs at critical checkpoints will bring in the required control mechanism to an independent AI system.

Apart from the human controls, a plethora of logical, fail-safe mechanisms can be incorporated into such systems. Establishment of a no-go checkpoint is one such idea. If a decision mechanism comes to such a decision, the automated checkpoint will trigger a nullification or a delay until it gets reviewed by an authorized human counterpart.

Not only in the field of technology, but also in regulatory frameworks and umbrella organizations are we seeing a gradual evolution to address these needs for establishing control. The Association for Computing Machinery has developed the annual, peer-reviewed Academic Conference on Fairness, Accountability, and Transparency. The conference focuses on the areas of algorithmic accountability, fairness, and so forth. Even the Federal Trade Commission Bureau of Consumer Protection in the United States is studying the impact of algorithms on consumer decisions by conducting and funding several studies in the area. The European Union also incorporated the "right to explanation" in its Data Protection Act in 2018, which highlights the requirement and obligation for maintaining transparency in algorithm-based intelligent systems.

Protect Access

With the rise in the adoption of AI technology, there is an even greater need to keep these technology advancements protected from being accessed by individuals or organizations with malicious intent. Enterprise IT systems are susceptible to malicious attacks or attacks from malicious ransomware. Bolstering the security mechanisms for such advanced technologies is of utmost importance.

Georgia Tech researchers have come up with one such solution to protect AI systems. The security method can detect and rectify distorted data classification, detect and rectify adversarial (malicious) data, and provide a score for the vulnerability/safety of any pretrained AI system. The researchers also developed a mechanism/apparatus that is capable of differentiating between normal and abnormal data for any AI algorithm, effectively detecting anomalies for pretrained AI algorithms, working on any type of data, and performing the task for any AI system as an add-on.[13]

Similar research is going on all over the world. Organizations using advanced AI systems are strengthening their defense systems to protect such systems from wrongdoers. Another factor that needs to be touched upon while discussing the protection of advanced technologies is *proprietorship*. Proper use of the existing patent laws can protect the proprietorship of such technologies. This harks back to our earlier discussion of ensuring accountability.

Over the next 10 years, organizations will be transformed, some of them dramatically, as they reorient themselves to a future in which they will innovate constantly and scale innovations repeatedly. To do this, they will invest in technologies, applications, and the people skills to develop and use them, and these will come together in complex, interconnected webs of capability. Machines, increasingly able to understand natural language and learn unassisted, will transcend their programming and evolve into more valuable resources to help them uncover new opportunities and create new solutions. Accelerating technology and adaptation in the way we interface with it will open up unprecedented areas for growth. Smart systems will become ever more pervasive and embedded in businesses and daily lives.

Building experience and competence in automation will matter more than ever as choices and capabilities expand. In a future consisting of organizations transformed by intelligent automation, the leaders who focused on this game-changing technology early will have allowed their companies to gain a serious competitive edge.

To state at the highest level the crucial work of managers in large enterprises, it is strategizing for the future, based on a point of view about how conditions will change. Intelligent automation will drive much of that change and will also respond to it. Throughout the ranks of organizations around the world, creative executives, managers, and workers must keep looking for new ways to exploit the power of intelligent automation. Many are already developing, piloting, and benefiting from ingenious solutions. They must keep injecting fresh energy into their efforts, building momentum, and taking their automation successes to scale.

Key Takeaways

- New generations of automation solutions will make the world better as long as they are guided by three core principles: relevance, resilience, and responsibility.
- Intelligent automation will gain greater *relevance* to enterprise success as it is increasingly applied to the problems and decisions that workers and customers care most about.
- With greater levels of awareness and adaptability, solutions will have more *resilience*—and will make enterprises themselves more resilient in response to unexpected setbacks and crises.
- Both vendors and users of intelligent automation solutions will build in greater *responsibility* by correcting for unethical biases, increasing transparency, ensuring controllability, and protecting access to these powerful systems.

NOTES

Preface

1. Information Age, "HFS Research: How Are Enterprise and Service Providers Coping with the Covid-19 Paradigm Shift?," April 8, 2020, https://www.information-age.com/hfs-research-how-are-businesses-coping-with-the-covid-19-paradigm-shift-123488895/.

Chapter 1

1. "Il Secolo XIX," Accenture Applied Intelligence Case Study, https://www.accenture.com/us-en/case-studies/digital/secolo-xix-building-better-journalism-ai.

2. Smriti Srivastava, "How Italy's Oldest News Daily Il Secolo XIX Embraced Applied Intelligence for Better Quality of Journalism," *Analytics Insight*, July 15, 2019, https://www.analyticsinsight.net/italys-oldest-news-daily-embraced-applied-intelligence-better-quality-journalism/.

3. David Noble, *Forces of Production: A Social History of Industrial Automation*, New Brunswick, NJ: Transaction, 2011, 66–67.

4. Derek Thompson, "Health Care Just Became the U.S.'s Largest Employer," *Atlantic*, January 9, 2018, https://www.theatlantic.com/business/archive/2018/01/health-care-america-jobs/550079/.

5. Gavin Weightman, "The History of the Bar Code," *Smithsonian*, September 23, 2015, https://www.smithsonianmag.com/innovation/history-bar-code-180956704/.

6. We have Peter Drucker to thank for the term *knowledge worker*, which he coined in 1959, a time when he was studying the workings of sprawling industrial organizations like General Motors. Peter F. Drucker, *Landmarks of Tomorrow*, New York: Harper, 1959. By the end of the twentieth century, it was very clear that Drucker had accurately predicted the trend. See James W. Cortada, *Rise of the Knowledge Worker*, Boston: Butterworth-Heinemann, 1998.

7. Paul R. Daugherty and H. James Wilson, *Human + Machine: Reimagining Work in the Age of AI*, Boston: HBR Press, 2018.

8. Forbes, "2020 Predictions About Automation and the Future of Work from Forrester," October 30, 2019, https://www.forbes.com /sites/gilpress/2019/10/30/2020-predictions-about-automation -and-the-future-of-work-from-forrester/?sh=a1965b71318a.

9. Nike, "New Live-Design Experience Promises Custom Shoes in Less Than 90 Minutes," news release, September 5, 2017, https:// news.nike.com/news/nike-makers-studio.

10. There is a rich literature devoted to the concept of Lean manufacturing, beginning with James Womack's classic *The Machine That Changed the World*, New York: Scribner, 1990, which introduced this new approach to operations management to the Western world. For a concise overview, see Pascal Dennis, *Lean Production Simplified: A Plain-Language Guide to the World's Most Powerful Production System*, 3rd edition, Boca Raton, FL: CRC Press, 2015.

11. Federal Bureau of Investigation, "Insurance Fraud," accessed September 27, 2020, https://www.fbi.gov/stats-services/publications /insurance-fraud#:~:text=The%20total%20cost%20of%20insurance ,the%20form%20of%20increased%20premiums.

Chapter 2

1. Ketan Awalegaonkar, Robert Berkey, Greg Douglass, and Athena Reilly, *AI: Built to Scale, from Experimental to Exponential*, Accenture survey report, 2019, https://www.accenture.com/_acnmedia /Thought-Leadership-Assets/PDF-2/Accenture-Built-to-Scale -PDF-Report.pdf.

2. This finding is in line with others' survey findings. An industry analyst firm, for example, recently highlighted the challenge of scaling. When it surveyed some 6,000 business leaders, it found great

enthusiasm for robotic process automation. Yet the majority of the respondents' RPA programs were limited to fewer than 10 robots, and fewer than 10 percent reported more than 100 robots up and running. Other studies, too, find many firms reporting active intelligent automation projects, but digging deeper, find that few of these are large, complex solutions, and only a tiny fraction of firms are implementing automation at scale.

3. See, for example, Joe McKendrick, "Artificial Intelligence Will Relieve Skills Shortages, If We Could Find Enough People to Build It," *Forbes*, May 16, 2018. It reports that 80 percent of business leaders surveyed cite a lack of talent to fill positions.

4. Cade Metz, "The Battle for Top AI Talent Only Gets Tougher from Here," *Wired*, March 23, 2017, https://www.wired.com/2017/03 /intel-just-jumped-fierce-competition-ai-talent/.

5. O'Reilly, AI Adoption in the Enterprise 2021 survey, April 19, 2021, https://www.businesswire.com/news/home/20210419005040 /en/As-Company-Culture-Warms-to-AI-Adoption-Lack-of-Skills -and-Difficulty-Hiring-Still-Present-Significant-Barriers-to-Entry -According-to-New-O%E2%80%99Reilly-Research.

6. Ellyn Shook and Mark Knickrehm, *Reworking the Revolution*, Accenture, 2018, https://www.accenture.com/_acnmedia/pdf-69 /accenture-reworking-the-revolution-jan-2018-pov.pdf.

7. Avanade, *Rethink AI Talent and Culture: The Secret Weapon to Scale AI for the Long Term*, Avanade research report, 2020, https:// www.avanade.com/-/media/asset/solutions/ai-talent-and-culture -research-report-.pdf?la=en&ver=1&hash=92AB22098DD650D9 E1124E2BBBCB8760.

8. CIO Insight, *Benefits and Challenges of Intelligent Automation*, 2017, https://www.cioinsight.com/it-management/slideshows/benefits -and-challenges-of-intelligent-automation.html.

9. Tadhg Nagle, Thomas C. Redman, and David Sammon, "Only 3 Percent of Companies' Data Meets Basic Quality Standards," *Harvard Business Review*, September 2017.

10. CBInsights, "The Top 100 AI Startups of 2019: Where Are They Now?" December 10, 2019, https://www.cbinsights.com/research /2019-top-100-ai-startups-where-are-they-now/.

11. David Kiron and Michael Schrage, "Strategy for and with AI," *MIT Sloan Management Review*, June 11, 2019, https://sloanreview .mit.edu/article/strategy-for-and-with-ai/.

12. In one survey of financial services industry executives, 43 percent of respondents reported this was true of their organizations. Capgemini Digital Transformation Institute, "Growth in the Machine: How Financial Services Can Move Intelligent Automation from Cost Play to Growth Strategy," July 11, 2018, https://www.capgemini .com/gb-en/resources/the-growth-in-the-machine.

13. Paul Daugherty, "The Post-Digital Era Is upon Us," Accenture research report, February 7, 2019, https://www.accenture.com/us -en/insights/technology/technology-trends-2019.

14. Economist Intelligence Unit, "The Advance of Automation: Business Hopes, Fears and Realities," briefing paper, 2019, https:// automationfirst.economist.com/wp-content/uploads/2019/06 /EIU-UiPath-The-advance-of-automation-briefing-paper.pdf.

Chapter 3

1. Gary Hamel and C. K. Prahalad, "Strategic Intent," *Harvard Business Review*, July-August 2005, 63–74, https://hbr.org/2005/07 /strategic-intent.

2. Accenture Technology Vision 2016, The Primacy of People in the Digital Age.

3. Elizabeth Doupnik, "Moda Operandi CTO: Machine Learning Crucial Asset for Business Growth," *Women's Wear Daily*, May 3, 2018, https://wwd.com/business-news/retail/moda-operandi-cto -q-a-1202662577/.

4. Gergana Mileva, "4 Brands Using Augmented Reality to Drive Immersive Customer Experiences," *AR Post*, August 7, 2019, https://arpost.co/2019/08/07/4-brands-augmented-reality-drive -immersive-customer-experiences/.

5. Carnegie Mellon University, Software Engineering Institute, Watts S. Humphrey Software Process Achievement Award site, https:// resources.sei.cmu.edu/news-events/events/watts/watts.cfm.

6. Jeff Dyer, Hal Gregersen, and Clayton M. Christensen, *The Innovator's DNA: Mastering the Five Skills of Disruptive Innovators*, Boston: Harvard Business Review Press, 2011.

Chapter 4

1. Lean process improvement is part of the larger set of methods called Lean manufacturing, which aims to create processes that run as efficiently, require as little slack, and incur as little waste as possible. Six Sigma is a methodology named for the term "six sigma quality" which means that a process is so well controlled that its variance is within process limits ±3s from the center line in a control chart, and its outputs fall within requirements/tolerance limits ±6s from the center line. This emphasis on getting consistently high-quality output from a production process informs the method's steps for studying and adjusting processes.

2. Root cause analysis grew out of a favorite practice by Toyota Industries founder Sakichi Toyoda (1867–1930), by which he used to ask "five whys" to go much deeper than the superficial identification of a problem and arrive at an understanding of its root cause. See Paul F. Wilson, Larry D. Dell, and Gaylord F. Anderson, *Root Cause Analysis: A Tool for Total Quality Management,* New York: ASQC Quality Press, 1993.

3. Penny Crosman, "How BNY Mellon Is Going Further on AI," *American Banker,* October 15, 2019. See also BNY Mellon's own research into robotic process automation and other technologies transforming financial services operations: *The Future of Payments: A Corporate Perspective,* 2018, https://www.bnymellon.com/content /dam/bnymellon/documents/pdf/articles/the-future-of-payments -a-corporate-perspective-report.pdf.

4. James F. Peltz, "Domino's Will Bring You Pizza by Robot, Drone or Canoe," *Chicago Tribune,* May 16, 2017, https://www .chicagotribune.com/business/ct-dominos-pizza-digital-tech -20170516-story.html.

Chapter 5

1. Maria Manuela Cunha, Bruno Conceicao Cortes, and Goran D. Putnik, *Adaptive Technologies and Business Integration: Social, Managerial and Organizational Dimensions,* Idea Group Reference, 2007, 33–58.

2. Victor R. Basili, Gianluigi Caldiera, and H. Dieter Rombach, "The Goal Question Metric Approach," 1994, http://www.cs.umd .edu/~mvz/handouts/gqm.pdf.

3. VeriSM™ is a service management approach from the organizational level, looking at the end-to-end view rather than focusing on a single department. It shows organizations how they can adopt a range of management practices in a flexible way to deliver the right product or service at the right time to their consumers. The not-for-profit International Foundation for Digital Competences owns and governs the VeriSM content and certification scheme. https://verism.global/faqs/.

4. Lafe Low, "CIO Interview with Patty Morrison, CIO and EVP Customer Support Services for Cardinal Health," *CIO Magazine*, February 16, 2018, https://www.cio.com/article/3256048/cio-interview-with-patty-morrison-cio-and-evp-customer-support-services-for-cardinal-health.html.

5. Accelerating Business Value with Intelligent Automation, Kofax Intelligent Automation Benchmark Study, 2019, https://www.kofax.com/-/media/Files/Reports/EN/rp_forbes-insights-accelerate-business-value-with-intelligent-automation_en.pdf?la=en&hash=29D2E8BC56D7BBB4A2D6A81BC522F0FFDAF67BC5.

6. Workplace Competence International, Ltd., *Handbook for New Members of Automation Project Steering Committees*, Hillsburgh, Ontario: WCI, 1986, http://www.roelfwoldring.com/resourcematerials/wcipdfquark/steer_handbook.pdf.

Chapter 6

1. Antoine Gara, "Wall Street Tech Spree: With Kensho Acquisition S&P Global Makes Largest A.I. Deal in History," *Forbes*, March 6, 2018, https://www.forbes.com/sites/antoinegara/2018/03/06/wall-street-tech-spree-with-kensho-acquisition-sp-global-makes-largest-a-i-deal-in-history/#49d5b86567b8.

2. For an excellent introduction to design thinking, see the book by the CEO whose firm (IDEO) pioneered the approach: *Change by Design: How Design Thinking Transforms Organizations and Inspires Innovation*, New York: HarperBusiness, 2009. For an enlightening exploration of how the concept applies specifically to business strategy and business model design, see Roger Martin, *The Design of Business: Why Design Thinking Is the Next Competitive Advantage*, Boston: HBR Press, 2009.

3. Rob Brodell, Jyoti Bhardwaj, Danthanh Tran, Eugene Ghimire, and Susan Price, "Using Empathy Interviews to Develop Customer-Centric Products," Capital One blog, https://www.capitalone.com/tech/software-engineering/using-empathy-interviews-to-develop-customer-centric-products/.

4. Thejournal.com, "Virtual Reality Headsets See Explosive Growth," July 1, 2021, https://thejournal.com/articles/2021/07/01/virtual-reality-headsets-see-explosive-growth.aspx.

5. "Accenture Develops Artificial Intelligence-Powered Solution to Help Improve How Visually Impaired People Live and Work," Accenture news release, July 28, 2017, https://newsroom.accenture.com/news/accenture-develops-artificial-intelligence-powered-solution-to-help-improve-how-visually-impaired-people-live-and-work.htm.

6. Scott Rosenberg, "Inside Salesforce's Quest to Bring Artificial Intelligence to Everyone," *Wired*, August 2, 2017, https://www.wired.com/story/inside-salesforces-quest-to-bring-artificial-intelligence-to-everyone/.

7. "Meet the Chinese Finance Giant That's Secretly an AI Company," *MIT Technology Review*, June 16, 2017, https://www.technologyreview.com/s/608103/ant-financial-chinas-giant-of-mobile-payments-is-rethinking-finance-with-ai/.

8. "Ant Financial—Pioneering China Fintech with Machine Learning," HBS student case study, https://digital.hbs.edu/platform-rctom/submission/ant-financial-pioneering-china-fintech-with-machine-learning/.

9. "Ant Financial to Share Full Suite of AI Capabilities with Asset Management Companies," press release, June 9, 2018, https://www.businesswire.com/news/home/20180619006514/en/Ant-Financial-Share-Full-Suite-AI-Capabilities.

10. Nathan Heller, "Estonia: The Digital Republic," *New Yorker*, December 11, 2017, https://www.newyorker.com/magazine/2017/12/18/estonia-the-digital-republic.

Chapter 7

1. Mark Muro, Robert Maxim, and Jacob Whiton, *Automation and Artificial Intelligence: How Machines Are Affecting People and*

Places, Washington, DC: Brookings Institution, 2019, https://www
.brookings.edu/research/automation-and-artificial-intelligence
-how-machines-affect-people-and-places/. Muro, a senior fellow at
Brookings, is quoted in Annie Nova and John W. Schoen, "Automation Threatening 25% of Jobs in the US, Especially the 'Boring
and Repetitive' Ones: Brookings Study," CNBC (website), January
25, 2019, https://www.cnbc.com/2019/01/25/these-workers-face
-the-highest-risk-of-losing-their-jobs-to-automation.html.

2. *Future of Production on Employment and Skills,* 2018, World Economic Forum.

3. Brent A. Kedzierski, "Moving Beyond Digital Transformation: The
Connected Worker at Shell," Intelligent Automation in Oil & Gas
Summit, International Quality and Productivity Center, 2020,
https://www.aiia.net/events-intelligent-automation-oil-and-gas
/downloads/moving-beyond-digital-transformation-the-connected
-worker-at-shell-with-brent-kedzierski?-ty-s.

4. World Economic Forum, *The Future of Jobs Report,* 2020, http://
www3.weforum.org/docs/WEF_Future_of_Jobs_2020.pdf.

5. Rob Goffee and Gareth Jones, *The Character of a Corporation,*
New York: Harper Business, 1998, 9. See also the classic work on
organizational culture, Edgar Schein, *Organizational Culture and
Leadership,* San Francisco: Jossey-Bass, 1992, 10.

6. NICE press release, "Independent Research Firm Finds 80 Percent
of Business Leaders Consider Robotic Process Automation Important to Improving," November 2019, https://www.bloomberg.com
/press-releases/2019-11-25/independent-research-firm-finds-80
-percent-of-business-leaders-consider-robotic-process-automation
-important-to-improving.

7. Aaron Hand, "Shell Gives Its Remote Workers a Heads Up," *Automation World,* April 4, 2019, https://www.automationworld.com
/products/software/blog/13319722/shell-gives-its-remote-workers
-a-heads-up.

8. BNY Mellon, "BNY Mellon's Automation Efforts Draw Industry
Accolades," press release, October 5, 2017, https://www.bnymellon
.com/us/en/about-us/newsroom/press-release/bny-mellons
-automation-efforts-draw-industry-accolades.html.

9. Dominic Delmolino and Mimi Whitehouse, "Responsible AI: A Framework for Building Trust in Your AI Solutions," Accenture Insights, 2018, https://www.accenture.com/_acnmedia/PDF-92/Accenture-AFS-Responsible-AI.pdf#zoom=50.

10. Soh Chin Ong, "Deep Water Safety Training Goes Virtual," Shell, https://www.shell.com/inside-energy/deep-water-safety-training-goes-virtual.html.

11. Edgar H. Schein, *Organizational Culture and Leadership*, 4th edition, Jossey-Bass, 2010, 305.

12. Avanade survey report, *What's Holding You Back?*, 2017, https://www.avanade.com/en-us/thinking/research-and-insights/-/media/asset/research/intelligent-automation-global-study.pdf.

13. Shook and Knickrehm, *Reworking the Revolution*, https://www.accenture.com/_acnmedia/PDF-69/Accenture-Reworking-the-Revolution-Jan-2018-POV.pdf.

14. Daugherty and Wilson, *Human + Machine: Reimagining Work in the Age of AI,* 166.

15. Sharon Gaudin, "At Stitch Fix, Data Scientists and A.I. Become Personal Stylists," Insider Pro, May 6, 2016, https://www.idginsiderpro.com/article/3067264/at-stitch-fix-data-scientists-and-ai-become-personal-stylists.html.

Chapter 8

1. John Kotter, "Why Do Change Efforts Lose Momentum?," *Forbes*, July 26, 2011, https://www.forbes.com/sites/johnkotter/2011/07/26/why-do-change-efforts-lose-momentum/#318b97b3396b.

2. Chip Heath and Dan Heath, *Switch: How to Change Things When Change Is Hard,* New York: Crown Business, 2010, 250, 251.

3. Marlene Jia, "Developing Hyperpersonalized Recommendation Systems (Interview with Jack Chua of Expedia)," Applied AI (podcast), https://appliedaibook.com/developing-hyperpersonalized-recommendation-systems-jack-chua-expedia/.

4. John Kotter, "Leading Change: Why Transformation Efforts Fail," Harvard Business Review, May/June 1995, https://hbr.org/1995/05/leading-change-why-transformation-efforts-fail-2.

5. Mariya Yao, Marlene Jia, and Adelyn Zhou, *Applied Artificial Intelligence: A Handbook for Business Leaders,* New York: Topbots, 2018, 55.

6. Kumar Chittipeddi, "Amazon's Empire Rests on Its Low-Key Approach to AI," CEO Advisory Services blog, April 12, 2019, https://www.ceoadvisoryservices.com/ceo-reads/2019/4/12/amazons-empire-rests-on-its-low-key-approach-to-ai.

Chapter 9

1. Ron Schmelzer, "The Fashion Industry Is Getting More Intelligent with AI," Cognitive World (blog), *Forbes*, July 16, 2019, https://www.forbes.com/sites/cognitiveworld/2019/07/16/the-fashion-industry-is-getting-more-intelligent-with-ai/.

2. Geoffrey G. Parker, Marshall W. Van Alstyne, and Sangeet Paul Choudary, *Platform Revolution: How Networked Markets Are Transforming the Economy and How to Make Them Work for You*, New York: W. W. Norton, 2016.

3. For a classic explanation of this phenomenon geared toward the general reader, see W. Brian Arthur, "Increasing Returns and the New World of Business," *Harvard Business Review*, 1996.

4. The notion that robust feedback systems can allow an entity to not only survive stress but actually strengthen and grow from being shocked by unforeseen and challenging stimuli is the thesis of a fascinating book: Nassim Nicholas Taleb, *Antifragile: Things That Gain from Disorder*, New York: Random House, 2014.

5. TechRepublic, "Forrester: Automation Could Lead to Another Jobless Recovery," May 8, 2020, https://www.techrepublic.com/article/forrester-automation-could-lead-to-another-jobless-recovery/.

6. Bernard Marr, "AI Can Now Copy Your Voice: What Does That Mean for Humans?," *Forbes*, May 6, 2019, https://www.forbes.com/sites/bernardmarr/2019/05/06/artificial-intelligence-can-now-copy-your-voice-what-does-that-mean-for-humans/#660828eb72a2.

7. Yavar Bathaee, "The Artificial Intelligence Black Box and the Failure of Intent and Causation," *Harvard Journal of Law & Technology* 31, no. 2 (Spring 2018), https://jolt.law.harvard.edu/assets/articlePDFs/v31/The-Artificial-Intelligence-Black-Box-and-the-Failure-of-Intent-and-Causation-Yavar-Bathaee.pdf.

8. Sarah Perez, "Microsoft Silences Its New A.I. Bot Tay, After Twitter Users Teach It Racism," *TechCrunch,* March 24, 2016, https://techcrunch.com/2016/03/24/microsoft-silences-its-new-a-i-bot-tay-after-twitter-users-teach-it-racism/.

9. Vivienne Ming, "Human Insight Remains Essential to Beat the Bias of Algorithms," *Financial Times,* December 3, 2019, https://www.ft.com/content/59520726-d0c5-11e9-b018-ca4456540ea6.

10. Ray Dalio, *Principles: Life and Work,* New York: Simon and Schuster, 2017, 100–101.

11. Ron Schmelzer, "Understanding Explainable AI," *Forbes,* July 23, 2019, https://www.forbes.com/sites/cognitiveworld/2019/07/23/understanding-explainable-ai/#278ac06b7c9e.

12. Filippo Santoni de Sio and Jeroen van den Hoven, "Meaningful Human Control over Autonomous Systems: A Philosophical Account," *Frontiers in Robotics and AI,* February 28, 2018, https://www.frontiersin.org/articles/10.3389/frobt.2018.00015/full.

13. G. AlRegib, M. Prabhushankar, G. Kwon, and D. Temel. "System and Method for Detecting and Protecting Against Deceptive Inputs for AI Systems and Measuring Vulnerabilities of Existing AI Systems," US Provisional Patent No. 62/899,783, September 2019, http://cantemel.com/patents/.

INDEX

Page numbers followed by *f* refer to figures.

ABOUT THE AUTHORS

Dr. Bhaskar Ghosh is Accenture's chief strategy officer, with responsibility for all aspects of the company's strategy and investments, including ventures and acquisitions and Accenture Research. He also oversees the development of all assets and offerings across Accenture's Services. In addition, Bhaskar has management responsibility for Industry X (digital manufacturing and intelligent products and platforms) and driving responsible business and sustainability services. He is a member of the Accenture Executive Committee and Global Management Committee.

Before being named to his current position in 2020, Bhaskar was advisor to the CEO on important topics, including growth and investment strategy, business performance, and organizational effectiveness and restructuring. Prior to that, he was the group chief executive of Accenture Technology Services with overall responsibility for the Accenture Application and Infrastructure Services business, directing strategy and investments, and leading platforms, products, and global technology delivery. In this role, he focused on enabling enterprises to drive growth through innovative technology services designed to reinvent their application strategy and portfolio.

Accenture Technology Services made outstanding progress to rapidly rotate to the new and enable clients to lead in the new under Bhaskar's leadership. More than 200,000 Accenture Technology people were trained around the world in new IT, including automation, Agile development, and intelligent platforms. In addition, Accenture strengthened new IT offerings around data, cloud, security, and liquid application management. In the same period, Accenture opened a ground-breaking Innovation Hub in Bengaluru with a focus on driving innovation at scale, and a network of more than 18 Liquid Studios around the world.

Bhaskar has personally provided leadership to develop cutting-edge technology solutions, including the technology automation platform, myWizard; Accenture's cloud assessment and migration platform, myNav; and the value-led ERP implementation platform of Accenture myConcerto. As an innovator, Bhaskar has been awarded six patents in the area of software engineering and platform development.

Bhaskar serves as an independent director on the Board of Directors of Housing Development Finance Corporation Limited (HDFC) and is chairman of its IT Strategy committee and a member of its Risk, Audit & Governance committee. Before joining Accenture in 2003, Bhaskar was vice president and global head of IT infrastructure management services at Infosys. Earlier in his career, he held several senior positions with Philips in India, where he worked extensively with the consumer electronics industry.

Bhaskar holds a bachelor of science degree and a master's degree in business administration from Calcutta University and a PhD in business management from Utkal University in India.